TRAVEL

EXPECT THE UNEXPECTED

TRAVEL

EXPECT THE UNEXPECTED

ALLAN BRODIE

atmosphere press

Travel. Expect the unexpected.

"When travel plans turn to dust, laugh.
You can always sue when you get home."

This is not a travel book. It is a humorous account of well-planned holidays gone awry. When embarking on a holiday, it doesn't matter how much you plan—there are some things you can't control. These stories are true experiences that will provide you with some valuable insights into travel, particularly the locations visited. However, you will not believe the things that actually go wrong. As soon as my family decides on a holiday location, I purchase a diary and enter all activities for each day, to ensure our days are full, interesting, and planned well in advance. One piece of advice: make sure you write the tour information on the correct day. I am not taking ownership of that mistake; after all, my wife was supposed to check it.

Whether it be incorrect information from the travel company regarding a pick-up time, a no-show from a taxi booked two months in advance, or your wife (because men can't read maps) taking you in the wrong direction and you walking double the distance you needed to, there are some things you can control. What you can't control are the cyclones, the earthquakes, and having dinner with vegans.

LONDON & GLASGOW, GREAT BRITAIN

My advice: expect the unexpected.

Ralph Waldo Emerson described London as "the epitome of our times, and the Rome of today."

It is so true. London is a major world influencer of business, technology, and learning through quality universities and prestigious secondary education. London is considered the epicentre of financial institutions and economic strategy, and the city is a player in decision-making affecting world affairs.

We were visiting London and Great Britain as tourists, so the technical importance of London was furthest from our minds. This was the late 1990s and pre our daughters' birth. My wife, Kerri, had never been to Britain before; however, this was my third visit. Consequently, I thought she should see it all in the five days we were there, and the diary I put together planned for that. Maybe a little too much. Each day was stacked with must-do's. Big Ben, Buckingham Palace, Portobello Rd., Abbey Rd., Piccadilly, and Trafalgar Square, just to name a few. Let's not forget the markets: Camden, Portobello, and Borough Market. In hindsight, the Hop on Hop off bus would have been a good option (or we could have just watched *Notting Hill* and *Love Actually*).

There was no time to dwell, as our plans—or should I say, my plans—were set in stone.

As we looked through the gates of Buckingham Palace, we looked at each other and burst into laughter. It reminded us of the time when a group of friends got together at our house to play Trivial Pursuit. When the question "Where does the Queen reside when in London?" came up, one of the girls jumped in almost before the question had been read out and answered, "Westminster Lobby." You can imagine that there

BIG BEN & HOUSES OF PARLIAMENT

was not a dry eye in the house.

I mentioned before that this was my third trip to Britain. I had some fond memories and some not so fond memories.

When I was fifteen, I travelled to Scotland to meet distant relatives. It was arranged for me to stay with my aunty, who was my grandmother's sister. She was bedridden and would bark orders from her bed, and everyone jumped. I was given my own room, but as I entered it for the first time, there was a strange musty scent that encompassed the whole space. I lay there with my eyes open and realized that it was dampness. Surely, I couldn't be subjected to this. As an asthma sufferer, I began to worry, until luckily, I met with my pen pal for lunch, an ex-beauty queen, and when I described my sleeping quarters, she ordered me to stay with her family. Who was I to argue?

On my second trip, I met a girl in Israel, on holiday from London. We got on extremely well—so well, in fact, that we arranged to meet up in London when we both returned, as I was based in Glasgow.

I am not sure if she really believed I would call her, but I did, and after a stunned silence on the other end of the phone, we arranged to meet for a coffee around the corner from her work. She seemed strange, reserved, and relatively cold—the complete opposite of when we were together in Israel. It turned out that she had a boyfriend. Oops!

As I had nowhere to stay, she got approval from her boss, an orthodontist, for me to sleep in the dentist's chair at the surgery in Knightsbridge. I woke up feeling like I had spent the night in a dentist's chair in Knightsbridge. I never saw her again.

Kerri and I hired a car and drove down to Bath and other towns in the Cotswolds. Absolutely beautiful. Again because of time constraints, we couldn't stop in the picturesque villages, where the streets were so narrow, they had double yellow lines on both sides of the road.

Back to London to embark on our five-day trip to Europe with Trafalgar Tours. We were staying at the Walkabout Club at the Elysee Hotel, which was frequented mainly by Australians, who used it as a home base. It was around $40 AUD per night back then, approximately £20, and was extremely clean, homely, and cheap, especially compared to other accommodations in the area. It was an unseasonably hot summer, and the hotel had no air conditioning, but we survived. We organized to leave our luggage at the hotel while we travelled across the channel to France. On our return, we had another two nights booked at the Elysee before heading off to Scotland.

When we reached Europe, we made a pact to try the traditional dishes of the cities we were going to visit, such as mussels in Brussels and escargot in France.

In Amsterdam, we tried a dish called stamppot, which included sausages, mash, and kale, which I wasn't that sure about. We also got dragged into an adult-only show by another couple on the tour. I am very broad minded, but I really didn't know where to look.

In a future story on Nouméa, I mention the fact that I

have a love for the French.

In Nouméa, I had learned 100 French words, but that had increased to about 200 by the time we arrived in Paris. We were walking along the Champs-Elysées with the tour group, when I suggested to my wife that we should split from the group and try a restaurant off the beaten track and away from the tourists. After all, I could speak fluent French now. She agreed, and we went down a couple of side streets until we found a quaint little restaurant.

We were greeted by the owners, a lovely older man and woman. Bonjour la nuit.

How good was this? We sat down and were handed the menus. I must have gone white because Kerri asked what was wrong. "It's all in French," I exclaimed. The only thing I recognized on the menu was the escargot (snails), and chateaubriand (steak), so I ordered two of each.

The only time, in my mind, that the woman realized we weren't French was when she said something after I had ordered the chateaubriand, and I took it to be how we wanted the steak cooked. I requested "well done" in English and she replied "No, No, No" and began pointing to the sole of her shoe.

Expect the unexpected.

We arrived back in London around 8:30 pm on Saturday evening. We went up to reception to re-check in, as we had a paid booking for our final two nights in London.

The girl on the desk looked somewhat stressed and a bead of sweat started to dribble down her forehead. We were advised that for some reason, our room had been double booked, and the only option was to share with six backpackers, me with the boys, and Kerri with the girls. I know it was only £20 per night, but I had paid that to be together, not apart. They apologized and stated that they had no other options, as they were fully booked.

I demanded they ring other hotels in the area, and I would

claim a refund on my return to Australia. The poor girl must have rung over ten hotels off her list, all of which were fully booked, until finally she found one around the corner with a vacancy.

She accompanied us and our luggage to our new place of residence for two nights, which was about 500 metres from the Elysee Hotel. We headed to the reception, walking past about six Indian gentlemen who were sitting smoking on makeshift benches, with all eyes following us, especially my wife. It was quite uncomfortable.

We were greeted by a very friendly lady who joined us in the lift, which was barely large enough to fit our luggage, let alone us as well.

We reached the top floor and were shown to our room. My wife was desperate to go to the toilet, and we noticed there was no toilet in the room. I could tell by the look she gave me that she wasn't happy. She departed and started heading down the hall. Just as she closed our door, the whole room shook. I thought it was an earthquake. It was so loud and made me feel a little unsteady on my feet. We were above the Underground.

Kerri returned soon after, with her face in this stunned, frozen look. The toilet was black with stains and whatever. OK, so we are not staying here. We grabbed our luggage, went back down the lift, passed the lovely lady and the six Indian gentlemen who had now become seven, and headed back to the Elysee Hotel

The receptionist could see us walking back in, and her face dropped, nearly as far as the floor. I was aware of no other hotels in London, apart from the one that Mum and Dad had stayed at a few times. Please ring the Waldorf, I said. Her face reminded me of paint being poured into a tray, dispersing evenly. I repeated my request. She rang the Waldorf, and they did have a vacancy. It was critical that we found a place to stay, as our next two days were fully booked, and my plans could not be altered. They could, actually, but my wife would've missed out on seeing something. She didn't care too much, but I did.

The receptionist put her hand over the mouthpiece of the phone and advised that it was £300 per night. With a raspy and nervous voice, I said I didn't care, just book it.

The taxi took us directly to the hotel; it was now just after 11 pm, and we were exhausted. I went up to reception, unshaven and looking like I had just been given some money for my first meal and board for weeks.

We reached the room and decided we would order room service in the morning so that we could get an early start. A continental breakfast, comprising of one croissant or bun, jam or marmalade, tea or coffee was £40 each or $80 AUD. Shocked and our finances about to take a big whack, I opened the blinds and saw a 'Wimpy Bar' across the road. Wimpy is a fast-food chain that is extremely affordable. Cheap. So that is where we had breakfast.

After more sightseeing in London, we headed to Hull and Leeds, to visit family members that we had never met before (you have to do this because your parents told you to, but also

DOUBLE DECKER BUS

because they think you will love meeting them).

As soon as we got over the border into Scotland, it was raining. We had pre-arranged with my Mum and Dad, who were also visiting, to pick them up and take them to a close family friend's house for lunch.

My father was a dominant soul, one that continually spoke down to you, and you never lived up to his expectations.

We arrived at the friend's house in a suburb of Glasgow called Whitecraigs. I could see the driveway stretching about fifty metres from the road up the house, where the family was all standing at their door, frantically waving. I am not very good at calculating elevation, but if we call the bottom sea level, the top had to be at least fifty metres away, not on a steady incline, but more on a steep incline. To make matters worse, there was no protection on either side. It was just a straight drop back to sea level.

So, I parked in the street. Of course, this wasn't good enough for my father. He called me everything under the sun, and everything over it as well, and requested I get out of the car so that he could get in. At full speed, as the hire car was lacking oomph, he shot up the driveway. What he hadn't seen, or planned on, was the slight curve in the driveway, about five metres from where our friends were still waving. Suddenly, his passenger side wheels went over the side.

The car was hanging precariously over the side. Dad got out of the driver's side, a little stunned and embarrassed, but Mum was stuck in the passenger side hanging over the edge.

Of course, she had to open the door and look down, didn't she?

As Kerri and I walked up the driveway towards the point of disembarkation, Dad looked at me, and I looked at him; I couldn't help but to direct a supercilious smile towards him.

Mum got out safely and it took two tow trucks to winch the hire car to safety. We visited the family on another two occasions, and Dad parked down in the street.

Scotland is beautiful, and for some reason, is often left off the itinerary when people visit the UK. The mountains of Aviemore, the grandeur of Edinburgh Castle, or the eerie mystery of Loch Ness. Please put Scotland on your bucket list.

For those of you who are lovers of soccer, I suggest a visit to either Celtic Park, home of the green and white hoops, or Ibrox Stadium, home to the Rangers Royal Blue. There is a fierce rivalry between them, so stay away if both teams are playing each other when you are there.

We made the mistake of driving up a side street past the ground just as some of the crowd were leaving after the game. The car started to rock from side to side, and I swear if I hadn't put my foot on the accelerator, we would have been left trying to get out of a car on its roof.

Expect the unexpected.

KELVINGROVE PARK

My five must sees and dos in London and Glasgow

1. Buckingham Palace

2. Big Ben

3. Bath

4. London Eye

5. Loch Ness Glasgow (A man went to take a photo of it to impress his mates. That was in 1963, and he is still waiting.)

MIAMI, FLORIDA, USA

My advice: expect the unexpected

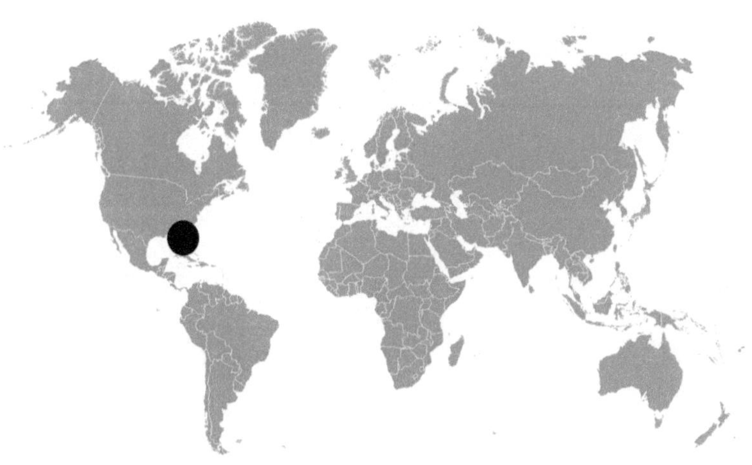

I was fortunate enough to win the 'Keith Graham' scholarship for the highest percentage growth in revenue in Australia for radio station advertising.

The prize consisted of airfares to New York, with accommodation and a ticket to a three-day conference. After discussing timing with my CEO, he decided that it would be beneficial to visit other states to enquire about how they have adapted to certain changes in the market that we were about to be exposed to.

I chose New Orleans, Miami, San Francisco, and of course, New York, and immediately contacted each of the relevant sales managers to organize an appointment.

The conference didn't appeal to me, but to have the opportunity to travel to these cities was quite exciting.

I had a month lead-up, but one afternoon, while working out in the gym in Canberra, one of my contacts joined me on the treadmill. He was an ex-diplomat and had spent time in Miami.

He warned me of the crime and shared tales about people who had been caught driving with their windows down; culprits would throw rabid animals into their cars and when they pulled over, would steal their car.

There were other instances where cars would stop at lights, and if their cars were unlocked, hijackers would try and steal their cars.

I started to question my decision to travel there. I was getting quite paranoid.

Miami was my first stop, and my brother, after hearing about the crime rate, suggested I stay in Fort Lauderdale, a safer tourist destination away from the city.

I thought about it, but I couldn't change my accommodation. I was still not sure if my contact was telling me the truth or not.

As I entered the hotel, two police guards were standing by the foyer entrance and they were heavily armed. Shivers went up my spine. As I checked in, reception warned me that it was forbidden to have 'ladies of the night' in my hotel room, especially as one guest had been found murdered in the lift a few weeks prior.

As I entered the lift to go to floor twelve, I read the sign stuck on the wall with Blu-Tack. It read 'Welcome to the... Hotel. Please refrain from smoking. Do not let strangers into your room. Do not answer the door unless you know who it is. If you have ordered room service, please confirm that they are hotel staff.' (How can I do that?) 'Have a nice day and welcome.'

Now I was really paranoid. I entered the room, and the warnings were posted inside the room as well. I decided to have a drink from the minibar and sat out on the balcony. All of a sudden, it occurred to me that a sniper could be getting prepared to 'take me out.' I quickly came back inside.

OJ Simpson's trial was on TV—so, I thought, well, it is too dangerous to go anywhere, I may as well order room service and watch the trial.

A chicken sandwich arrived from room service, after clarification that it was really them. I sat on the bed all afternoon, feeling like I was serving a prison sentence, but through good behaviour, I got a TV.

I had already booked a Key West sea adventure and thought it would be hard to shoot me if I am out in the ocean. I turned up to the docks, and found the boat and tour group. I was extremely nervous but thought, I can do this. After all, I had seen *Finding Nemo*. I put on my goggles and snorkel, and down I went. I felt safer than I had in the previous twenty-four hours. It was like being in a dream. Surrounded by fish, going about their everyday life as if they had not a trouble in the world. And I felt the same way. Until I saw a shark coming towards me. It wasn't that big, but it was a shark. At speed, I swam 100 yards in record time. Reached the boat, and scrambled into it, banging my knee on the hull as I climbed in. The crew must've witnessed this and asked if I was OK. I replied that I had seen a shark. "Oh, that's Edward," they said. "He comes to visit every day."

BEAUTIFUL MIAMI BEACH

The next day, I felt no different. Quite uneasy, if I was being truthful. Even though I had been swimming with sharks the day before, I had taken a taxi directly to the wharf and one straight back home. I had not really ventured outside, if you will. The following morning, I had breakfast in the hotel and watched more of the OJ Simpson trial. I also decided to do some work to fill in time. I had a short snooze to alleviate the jet lag, which certainly helped.

Just then, I looked out the window and saw an old lady walking with her grocery trolley. You know, the type that has four wheels, with a vinyl cover that goes over the top. I thought to myself, how dangerous could it be if she was out and about? I went down to reception and asked whether it was safe to go outside. She replied, of course, but suggested that I shouldn't do it after nightfall.

There was a market around the corner, and the atmosphere was sensational. Most of the traders were Cubans because of the proximity to Cuba, and the goods on offer were very different and very much influenced by that country. Boots, leather jackets, shoes. It had a great variety.

I returned to the hotel and ordered room service for dinner. I was watching the news when a news flash broke into the normal programming. Gangs were involved in a shooting at Fort Lauderdale beach; the news showed youths firing at others, with sunbathers on beach towels, cowering, trapped in the middle.

The following morning, I took off to visit the radio station. The driver had the radio on. WZTU Miami is a Spanish contemporary music station. The nine o'clock news came on, with not-so-interesting news, but then they crossed to Barry in the WZTU chopper. With a Spanish accent mixed with a slightly Southern drawl, Barry said, "Thanks, Chuck. We are just travelling over the main highway just past Southwest Coconut Grove.

Everything seems to be moving well, Chuck. There are no hold-ups on Biscayne Boulevard, and traffic is flowing well on Ocean Drive. However, the traffic does slow around the Franklin Ave off-ramp, where there was a fatal shooting about thirty minutes ago, so best to avoid that and perhaps take the off-ramp at Ariete instead. Otherwise, all is good on the roads, Chuck."

I got out of Miami, as quickly as I could.

My five must sees and dos in Miami

1. Everglades Airboat Drive
2. Skyline Cruise
3. Little Havana Food and Walking Tour
4. Harbour Dinner Cruise
5. Key West Snorkelling Tour

NEW YORK, NEW YORK STATE, USA

My advice: expect the unexpected.

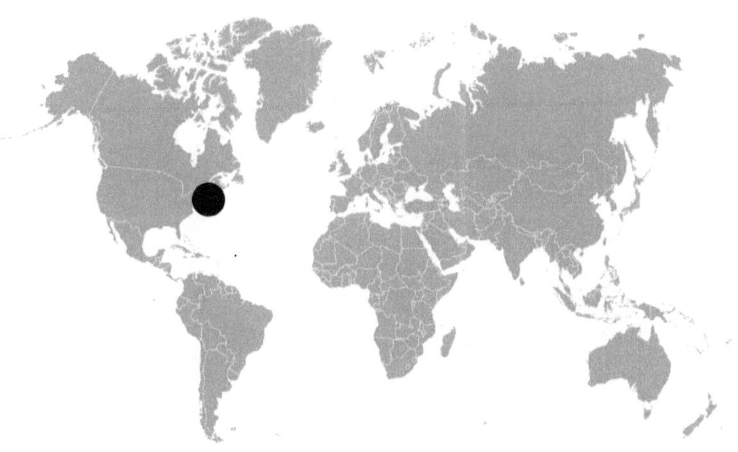

New York was much more civilized than Miami in my opinion. I visited during Giuliani's reign and it was much safer than it had been. It was February, so winter had definitely set in. I stayed in the Sheraton Times Square and when Kerri joined me two years later, we stayed at the Algonquin. Both were great hotels but were different in every way. The Sheraton was modern and had a gym facing the street at ground level, where you could watch everyone heading off to work. I love people-watching.

The Algonquin, on the other hand, is a hotel at 59 West 44th Street in Midtown Manhattan. The 181-room hotel opened in 1902 and has hosted numerous literary and theatrical notables throughout its history, including members of the Algonquin Round Table Club during the early twentieth century.

Being winter, Central Park's lake was frozen, and Kerri took the opportunity to ice skate there. What a serene experience, watching my wife ice skating in Central Park, with the multistory buildings and apartment blocks in the background. Rockefeller Square was another option for the public to ice skate. We had been warned not to look like tourists or open maps in the middle of the streets. We looked so unlike tourists, four people asked us for directions.

We spent our time efficiently in New York, visiting the tourist landmarks such as the Empire State Building, Times Square, Broadway, and the ferry across to Staten Island and the Statue of Liberty. This city was different now since Rudy Giuliani was focused on making it safer. Unfortunately, he won't be remembered for that, as recent events have clouded the water. I can still see the dye in his hair running down his forehead from the sweat at a Trump press conference.

I love shopping, so we walked from 3rd Avenue along 59th Street up to 5th Avenue and then down 58th, then 57th, and so on until we reached 52nd Street. Sale. Sale. Sale. We entered Bloomingdale's from the back street and went straight into the menswear department, which was lucky, because if we had entered into women's wear, we would have never gotten out. Anyway, there was a rack of suits with a 50% off sign. I started searching for my size and found an Armani in a light green. I loved it, but it was $2400 USD. Too much for my wage bracket. However I noticed that the $2400 was crossed out, which made me think that this meant 50% off. I got it for $200 USD.

I think because it had been there a while, they kept discounting it. I still have it. It doesn't fit, but I won't let it go. I might even ask to be buried in it.

We met with some very close relations, or so we were told. They were my grandmother's sisters' daughters' daughters. Mmmmm. They were nice to have picked us up from the

NEW YORK CITY

airport after returning from Syracuse, but they argued and argued about what route to take, whether they were going too fast or too slow, until finally we ended up at the Second Ave deli.

It was amazing, with all the varieties of real New York food. Reuben sandwiches, hot corned beef sandwich, chopped liver, and matzoh ball soup.

We also went to see *Phantom of the Opera* on Broadway. Kerri coughed all the way through. It was so embarrassing. It's funny how whenever you want to stop something or refrain from doing something, it happens and there is nothing you can do to stop it.

Many limit their trip to New York City alone, but New York State offers something very different. We had a few days at Syracuse, where snow covered every inch of ground, a picture that I had only seen before in movies.

Our work colleague, who I had built up a friendship with

SYRACUSE

on his visit to Australia, picked us up from our hotel and took us out for breakfast. On our way, he stopped for some bread. We got out of the car and walked gingerly through the snow. The shop keeper asked our friend what we were doing, to which he replied, "They have never seen snow before," which was correct.

We didn't see a lot of Syracuse, because we spent most of the time indoors, as we weren't used to the cold. February in New York is not for everyone. However, Chuck did take us to see the Syracuse Cathedral and the Diana Fountain.

My five must sees and dos in New York

1.   Empire State Building

2.   Central Park

3.   9/11 Memorial

4.   Statue of Liberty and Staten Island Cruise

5.   Times Square

NEW ORLEANS, LOUISINA, USA

My advice: expect the unexpected.

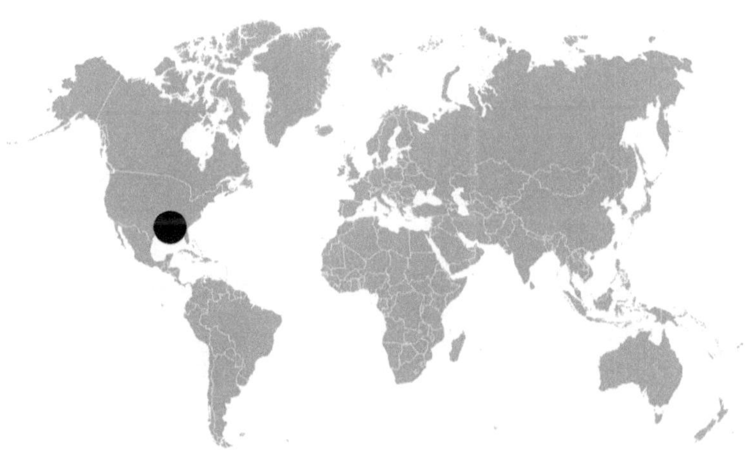

FAMOUS BOURBON STREET NEW ORLEANS

Bourbon Street. That's all you need to say. It is so famous, that for many visitors, Bourbon Street embodies the life of a party town.

The street is lit up by neon lights, with all types of music played from one bar to the next. As you walk down the street, each music genre can be heard, and it's more effective than changing vinyl records on the record player. Entry is free, but you are expected to buy a drink while you are sitting inside, admiring the quality of each performer.

Interaction with the performer and the punters is very common. One evening, we were having dinner at a Louisiana-themed restaurant, and I was called up to play the washboard. It was very funny and so was my washboarding.

Safety is still an issue in New Orleans, as you are advised to stay within the French Quarter.

Another hot spot for fun and action during Mardi Gras is Canal Street. Up to a million people crowd into every square inch of the parade route to enjoy the festivities for which New Orleans is internationally renowned.

Flooding, exacerbated by the reclaiming of salt marshes and bayous, is a huge issue, as is the fact that the land is below sea level. We were there pre-Katrina and our thoughts go out to all of those who lost their lives and livelihoods.

We went on a tour that began down a side street, where all of a sudden, we looked up only to see a ship sailing past. We were below sea level.

The vibe in New Orleans is second to none. The bars stretch across every piece of land. Exciting and professional entertainers, that you swear could relegate the Boss, to a support act.

The fact is that no one could say that they didn't enjoy New Orleans.

I cannot remember when the bars open, but we were visiting them quite early, just to hear the music. However, as they made no money from you sitting there watching the entertainment, you were expected to buy a drink. At 10 am, my palate couldn't take it, so a Coca-Cola was the best I could do.

By the time we hit most of the bars along Bourbon St., I had consumed over eight glasses of Coca-Cola before noon.

STREET CAR IN NEW ORLEANS

We found our own way to Jackson Square, which was formerly known as

Place d'Armes, a historic park in the French quarter. My wife, Kerri, talked me into a horse and carriage ride, which gave us good exposure to entertainers like jugglers, musicians, and other forms of local entertainment as we rode through the French Quarter.

I was quite happy to just visit bars and enjoy the street music, but Kerri wanted to sightsee. After all, I was getting very bloated after drinking so much Coca-Cola.

We visited the Oak Alley Plantation, where the driveway had a long line of beautiful trees adjacent to each other providing a sovereign type entrance.

The tour then took us through swampland to view wildlife such as alligators and snakes. I was hoping that one of the alligators didn't recognize my belt.

New Orleans people are very superstitious. Many shops, cafes, and restaurants have voodoo dolls on display, as well as shops selling them. On our second day in New Orleans, I felt a sharp pain in my back. It appears that my wife, Kerri, had bought a voodoo doll and was sticking knives in its back.

My five must sees and dos in New Orleans

1. Bourbon Street

2. Any Bar

3. National WWW 2 Museum

4. Jackson Square

5. St. Louis Cathedral

SAN FRANCISCO, CALIFORNIA, USA

My advice: expect the unexpected.

We checked in to a beautiful hotel, quite close to the wharves. As we started unpacking, I decided that we should see reception about booking a tour. As I grabbed the door handle, it fell off in my hand. Alas, there was no phone in the room. We also had made the decision not to bring our mobile phones on this holiday, for security reasons. I could just see us stuck in the room until the following morning when the cleaners were scheduled. We started knocking on the door in the hope that someone would hear us. Then it became a thump, until my knuckles were hurting. Kerri looked out the window, and if you strained, there was another window from the room next door around the corner. She saw a shadow and started waving and yelling, until the shadow reacted. The guy opened his window, and Kerri was able to convey our issue, and he rang reception on our behalf. They had a locksmith there that afternoon.

First stop after a false start from pit lane was Pier 39 and lunch.

You would have to go a long way, and some, to taste a better Clam Chowder than that available at the San Francisco docks, Pier 39. It's served in a loaf of bread, with the insides removed to create a cave-like hole and an excuse to lick the bowl afterward.

The wharf is a hub of activity, with many different cuisines available at the large selection of restaurants. Be careful of the seagulls while you are eating your dinner. They tend to try and get the meal without paying. Same for the seals, who nestle in on the buoys. You can smell them a mile away.

San Francisco has many sights to see. We travelled to

Haight-Ashbury, birthplace of the '60s revolution, with its ever-changing music, testing the standards set by the more conservative and their set-in-their way habits. Sex, drugs, and rock 'n' roll. To be there standing on the corner next to the sign was quite surreal.

I can remember my flairs and platform shoes. As I am scared of heights, I wonder how I got away with them. The '60s and '70s were great eras, and they started here in San Francisco.

We caught a taxi to the "Painted Ladies," a row of Victorian houses at Steiner Street across from Alamo Square Park. They are also known as the Seven Sisters. The houses were built between 1892 and 1896 by developer Matthew Kavanaugh, who lived next door in the 1892 mansion. This block appears very frequently in media and mass-market photographs of the city and its tourist attractions and has appeared in an estimated seventy movies, TV programs, and ads.

We decided to walk the three km back to Fisherman's Wharf through the park and some of the side streets. On our return to the hotel, when we were asked if we had a nice day, we talked about our lovely walk back. The concierge advised that was something we probably should not do again, due to the neighborhoods we had walked through.

We joined a tour group to travel across the water to Alcatraz Island, once home to one of the USA's most revered penitentiaries. The boat trip was only two km offshore from San Francisco.

The audio was well worth the extra because, at every nook and cranny, you could hear voices and sounds, as they would have been back then. A very eerie feeling indeed, and because of its isolation and its location in the cold waters and strong currents of San Francisco Bay, prison operators believed Alcatraz to be escape proof.

Since our trips to the States, we have become avid watchers of TV shows such as *The Streets of San Francisco*, *Charmed*, Full *House*, and some great movies, all filmed in San Francisco, such as *Vertigo*, *The Maltese Falcon*, *Guess Who's Coming to Dinner*, *Dirty Harry*, and *The Matrix*.

The roads were as they appeared in these films and you felt the incline in your quad muscles and calves.

We tried the tram on one occasion, and it certainly is a great transport alternative.

Sausalito was a recommendation, so on our last day we decided to take the bus on the twenty-five-minute trip. We rode across the bridge, which was an experience in itself.

We bought fish and chips and ate on the waterfront promenade, admiring all the old wooden houseboats.

It was worth the trip.

THE PAINTED LADIES

My five must sees and dos in San Francisco

1. San Francisco Wharf Pier 39
2. The Painted Ladies
3. Alcatraz
4. Golden Gate Bridge Tour
5. All the 'bloody' seagulls

PENANG, MALAYSIA

My advice: expect the unexpected.

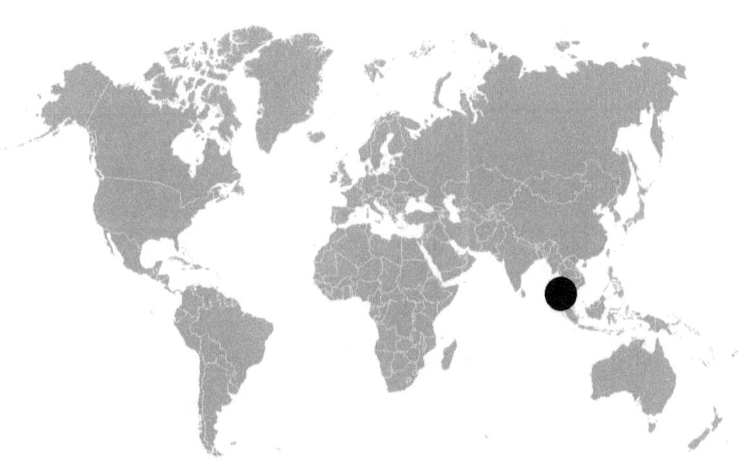

Penang is a small idyllic island state located on the northwest coast of Malaysia, and is only one hour flying time from Kuala Lumpur.

Our daughter Tara was five years of age when we visited Batu Ferringhi Penang. Ten nights of sunbathing in pristine waters, white sand and toned and tanned bodies. Well, the white sands and pristine waters was true.

As we planned our holiday and chose our hotel, the rest was easy, apart from asking ourselves "Do we prebook a private transfer or just share a hotel shuttle with other guests?"

Sometimes saving money is not always the correct decision. As we wound our way through the forests and ascended up and descended down the hills towards our resort and the beach, all of a sudden Tara projectile vomited over the couple in front. It was so embarrassing. I offered them my handkerchief to clean the back of their heads, and to pay for their dry cleaning, but they were very nice about it and politely refused. They happened to be staying at our resort, and every time we saw them coming around the corner, we hid. Next time, we are getting private transport.

Each day went past with perfect weather and pristine waters and white sand. I only repeat myself because that's what it felt like. It was beautiful, but I am just not a lie on my back and swim in the ocean every day kind of guy.

The only change to the scenery was when we saw women in full hijab, skydiving to the ocean below, and woke to the sounds of prayers from either the Muslim or Buddhist church next door, complete with microphone.

This occurred at six o'clock every morning.

My wife, Kerri, could sense this. Something to do with me complaining every minute of every day.

She suggested we go 'glam camping' and handed me a brochure on Boulder Valley and Hillside Retreat, both glam camping experiences in Penang. I thought, I reviewed, and I said no.

My last experience camping was not a good one. Five years previously, we had decided to go camping for the first time in Melbourne, Australia. I visited the camping store and left with a brand new five-man tent, a foldaway table and chairs for four people, a cast iron jaffle maker, three headlights, two cast iron skillets, a cast iron damper pot, three sleeping bags, and three blow-up Lilo beds. I couldn't see myself going to the toilet in the bush, so I booked a cabin with a backyard, and made Kerri and Tara promise that we couldn't go into the cottage unless we needed to go to the toilet or to have a shower.

We arrived at our destination, which turned out to be only thirty minutes from our home. It took ages to get everything out of our car, probably longer than the trip itself. With the help of our twelve-year-old daughter, we set up the tent, with price tags and all. It was now lunch time, and our menu of sausages in bread had been decided beforehand.

After cooking the sausages to perfection on the open fire, we ate, and with satisfied stomachs, looked at each other, wondering why we had never decided to camp before. Just then, the clouds came over and the heavens opened up, and we rushed to take cover in our brand new five-man tent.

We zipped the tent up to ensure we didn't get any wetter, then we sat in the tent waiting for the rain to stop.

The rain lasted approximately two hours, and when we unzipped the tent and stepped out, we were faced with mud, mud, and more mud. One of the polystyrene Eskys had lost its lid; a quarter of it was filled with water and all of the matches and firelighters were completely soaked. We emptied the water, and I suggested that I visit the cabin to go to the toilet, when really I was going searching for more matches and firelighters, which I found.

I started the fire again, and we sat there in our damp clothes. It was now 5 pm, so we decided it was time for dinner, considering there wasn't much else to do. Ham and cheese sandwiches in the jaffle iron were fantastic. We made the damper and put the cast iron pot in the fire. At 6 pm, it was completely dark, so we decided to go to bed, as the chill of the night was beginning to kick in, this time ensuring the other Esky containing breakfast and the cottage's matches and fire-lighters were secure.

I am not sure what time it was, as Kerri, Tara, and the dog, Molly, were fast asleep, but I needed to have a toilet stop. Trying to be careful and quiet as not to wake them, I put on my headlight and started to unzip the tent. I tried placing my feet outside the tent and attempted to put on my boots, so that they wouldn't trample mud through the tent. One foot outside the tent, and one foot inside, if that makes sense. Just then, I noticed a shadow on the top of the tent. It was a hunts-man spider on the roof with a leg span of around five inches. They are harmless, but not when they scare the living bejesus out of you. I fell back and landed on the other Esky, breaking

SUSPENSION BRIDGE IN PENANG NATIONAL PARK

the polystyrene, and all the food, matches, and firelighters fell into the mud.

At 6 am, we packed up and went home, not before finding our charcoal damper that we forgot to retrieve out of the fire. Glam camping? Don't even think about it! Happy to just lie on the beach and sunbake.

My five must sees and dos in Penang

1. Georgetown

2. Rainbow Skywalk and Observatory

3. Glam Camping

4. Balik, Pulau

5. Temple Tour

INSURANCE
Do I or don't I?

My advice: expect the unexpected.

So many choices. Where do I begin? Do I really need it? It will never happen to me. Is the $250 cover too expensive or too light on?

These are the questions I asked myself a few years ago. After all, I had travelled so many times, and nothing had ever gone wrong. We booked our Hawaii holiday twelve months in advance, and it was for this reason that I decided to take out cover.

Expect the unexpected.

Over a period of a few days, I started to get quite bloated. Even though I was in pain, I do have a habit of drinking carbonated soft drinks, so felt that it was just wind. After two weeks of being uncomfortable, I decided to visit my gastroenterologist, who luckily had a cancellation for the next week. She booked me in for a colonoscopy and gastroscopy, and I started preparation. To this day, I cannot believe that a COVID vaccine was created in six months, yet the taste of this bowel preparation liquid still cannot be improved.

Anyway, both results were clear. The gastroenterologist then suggested that I swallow a small camera, to provide her with a more detailed look at my stomach. I felt a little uncomfortable when she first mentioned it and advised that it would pass within a few days.

My daughter Tara accompanied me to the hospital to have the camera digested. After I swallowed it, I asked Tara to smile, and I bent over and pretended to take her photo.

She didn't think it was funny. I am just glad it wasn't a Polaroid. I was lucky that all was clear.

This was my first experience that confirmed our choice

to take out insurance, although such a common occurrence could've been assessed as a preexisting condition.

The second one was worse.

Hawaii was all booked and paid for, although Booking.com allowed us grace up to a certain date for free cancellation. It was our first venture to Hawaii as a family (I had been there for a conference many years prior), so we weren't entirely sure what to expect. Spending $250 for cover seemed like a waste of money, as I was relatively healthy, until one night.

I was starting to go off to sleep after an extremely tiring day at work. My wife was in the bathroom taking off her makeup and getting ready for bed. Unbeknown to me, I had a brain bleed from a burst cavernoma, a rare condition where a blood vessel bursts.

Kerri turned off the bedroom light and entered the bedroom in darkness. As she positioned herself under the blankets, she felt the bed shaking as if an earthquake had hit and we were caught in the epicentre.

She thought I was joking, as I tended to do, and kicked me, but to no avail. She turned on the light to see blood all over the pillow, and me in the middle of a seizure. Unfortunately, our daughter Tara came into the room to see what the commotion was.

Of course, I was completely oblivious to any of this as she telephoned emergency and in panic mode requested an ambulance.

It wasn't until the following morning that I awoke in ICU, with tubes coming out and going into all parts of my body. Believe me, our Hawaii trip was not the first thing on my mind.

After consultations with doctors and visits from the family, it became apparent as to what had occurred.

A brilliant and well-known neurosurgeon decided that we needed to operate, to clear the internal bleeding and remove the risk of another seizure.

I woke up forty-eight hours later and was advised that all had gone according to plan, and within hours was moved into a two-bed shared ward in the neurology department.

Forty-eight hours after the operation, I was feeling OK, although the staples on my head were a little uncomfortable. The Scottish accented nurse asked if I would be OK if she took my roommate from the other bed down to be discharged. Of course, I had no problem with that. I was going to get my own room. Lunch arrived, and I was excited because it was my first meal since the operation, and my favourite spaghetti to boot.

Expect the unexpected.

I took a couple of mouthfuls but started to feel strange. Just then, my wife and daughter arrived for visiting hours and they noticed that I was having difficulty breathing.

As an asthma sufferer, this was not unusual, so Kerri gave me two puffs of my Ventolin.

My breathing, or lack of it, deteriorated more, and the pain in my chest got worse. I started to panic.

Kerri immediately deduced that I was having a heart attack.

She ran to the nurses' station and alerted them to the problem. One of the nurses returned with a cardiac machine and attempted to stick the electrodes onto my chest.

Unfortunately, my chest was too hairy, making it impossible for the electrodes to stick.

The nurse left the room again, this time in a panic, just to make us feel comfortable, I suppose.

While she was away, Kerri and Tara were standing there with their mouths open, in clear distress. Another nurse entered the room and started to remove the machine, as she had another use for it.

Not a smart thing to do in front of my wife, and she retreated after being told in no uncertain terms that I was having a heart attack.

I was in agony. The nurse returned with a blade and shaved

an area, allowing for the electrodes to stick. Unfortunately, I had gone into the next stage, which included sweating, again making her actions more difficult.

My little Scottish nurse arrived back and could not believe what had happened whilst she was discharging the other patient.

Finally, the neurosurgeon heard the code blue or yellow (I'm not sure what it was because I'm colourblind), came in, and took complete control, as well as comforting Kerri and Tara.

Hawaii was still the furthest from my mind. The medical team wanted to conduct an angiogram to confirm their diagnosis, because of my recent brain bleed. This meant that I was in the hospital for three weeks before they gave it the all-clear.

A double bypass ensured, after they discovered two blocked arteries, one at 90%.

When I came out of the operation, I was in enormous pain. It was my birthday, but I was in no mood to open presents. Kerri sat with me, holding my hand and assuring me that I would be fine.

The hospital was at breaking point. Many patients, including me, were placed in a temporary ICU unit in one of the corridors, separated only by curtains, meaning that sleeping was not an option. To this day, I can still remember the 'ker thump, ker thump' of trolleys hitting a metal cover on the floor on the other side of the curtain.

Pain killers were also in shortage, or so we thought. Nurses from agencies were trying to handle the overload, and finally after three requests from Kerri and an hour of waiting in pain, I received them. After the operation, the procedure continued with rehab, and now I have a nice little bump on my pectoral where a pacemaker was inserted.

Thank god for insurance. I still had to jump over some hoops as they questioned whether it was a preexisting illness, but we got there in the end.

Expect the unexpected. You never know.

By the way, Hawaii was great, a surfer's paradise on steroids. That, however, is a tale for another day.

53

HAWAII, OAHU,
STATE OF HAWAII, USA

My advice: expect the unexpected.

HAWAIIAN LUAU AT SUNSET

I describe Hawaii, in particular Waikiki, as a beach resort on steroids. We have visited four times since 2005, and found something to do differently on each. We have always stayed at the Outrigger on Waikiki, mainly because it is home to Duke's, one of the most famous bars/night spots in Hawaii. Sunday afternoons are the best. A local band plays while you sip your afternoon cocktail.

Waikiki is similar to the smaller Pacific islands, but the shopping on the main strip, Kalakua Avenue, is to die for. Running adjacent to the beach, but sheltered by five-star hotels, Kalakaua Avenue is also known as the Rodeo Drive of the Pacific. My daughter and wife booked a swim with the turtles tour, and on return, said it was one of the best things they have ever done. It was called Turtle Canyon, and by all reports, was the best location out of all of the tours, and reputedly, one of the best in the world. These were green turtles, and all you needed to do was put your face in the water to experience the turtles swimming up to you without a care in the world.

Everything was going well, and the surf was up, until Kerri, who is extremely sure-footed—apart from falling down the stairs at our hotel in Hong Kong, tripping on the footpath in Melbourne, and falling with a thud over the tram separators in Barcelona—felt the force of a wave, which turned her upside down and onto her head.

That afternoon, we were sure she had concussion, so we decided to visit the DFO. Approximately forty minutes away by bus, the Waikele Premium Outlets are like no other.

Brand names are available at heavily reduced prices. If you arrive at the right time of the year, you can benefit from extra sales, sometimes as much as 50% off.

Whether she still had concussion or not, Kerri had circled all shops and reached the end; she was with Tara, and they'd made it around the circuit without reaching for their wallets. The bus was due to leave in fifteen minutes, but instead of getting there early to get a good seat, the girls visited a Gap store.

The bus leaves at certain times, so with notice, you can stay longer. Not my wife and daughter. They went ballistic. Trying on clothes, sorting out clothes, and paying for clothes— all within the fifteen minutes that I was waiting for the bus.

Pearl Harbor is a tour I would highly recommend. Bookings are essential. Tours include the USS Arizona Memorial, which is extremely moving and emotional. The USS Missouri Battleship is another must. We were lucky enough to see a team of US Marines training on the boat, only to find out that they were off to Iraq within days. I felt so loyal to them as an Australian, and offered my thanks to a couple of the Marines.

You walk across a bridge and over the USS Arizona. It is a surreal moment, but also an eerie one. No matter what country you were born in, this is a very solemn moment.

Don't rush these tours. In fact, I made Tara watch the old film *Tora! Tora! Tora!* before we left home, to give her some background into why and how this disaster happened.

On our last visit, we decided to book a tour of the northern beaches, where most of the surfing competitions are held.

On a Wednesday morning about six o'clock, we were sound asleep and were woken by reception. We were advised that the driver had arrived to take us to the northern beaches.

We thought it was the next day. We rushed to get dressed and do our teeth, and were downstairs within fifteen minutes, which was a good get, as Tara normally takes one hour to get ready. The driver was a little unhappy, but off we went. It was pouring rain, which immediately put a dampener, pardon the pun, on our visit to some of the best beaches in the world. Our first stop was a car wash, which was interesting, as we were paying for his time, but we were too scared to say anything. We were sitting there quietly and I remembered a time when my father asked one of his employees to take his car to get it washed. About an hour later, he returned, absolutely soaked. His suit, his shirt, and his tie.

We asked him what had happened. He told us that he had turned the car off in the car wash, but had left the windows down. As the engine was off, the electric windows didn't work, so he placed his back and backside up to the window in an attempt to stop the water from coming into the car.

Anyway, off we went, and our next stop was Giovanni's shrimp truck. Established in the 1930s, Giovanni's is known for its garlic prawns. Even though this isn't a dish we would normally have for breakfast, it was time to make an exception. In the rain, and on cardboard trays, the prawns melted in our mouth. That turned out to be the highlight of our northern beaches tour. It continued raining all day, which precluded us from seeing any of the beaches or any of the landmarks.

Still, we had booked dinner in the revolving restaurant. The view over Waikiki was exceptional, as was the food. The only issue I had was after I went to the toilet; when I got back, I couldn't find our table, as it had rotated 180 degrees. I thought the family had taken flight. I must also mention the shave ice, which is available on most corners. The ice absorbs the flavoured syrup, without it ending up in the bottom of the cup.

It is well worth a try.

My five must sees and dos in Hawaii

1. Northern Beaches

2. Waikiki

3. Pearl Harbor

4. Swim with the Turtles

5. Waikele Premium Outlets

TOKYO & KYOTO, JAPAN

My advice: expect the unexpected.

After arriving in Tokyo, via a stopover in Singapore, our first experience in this magical city was with our first meal, breakfast. Breakfast Japanese style. It was free in the hotel but now we know why. Rice, meat, and we weren't sure what else wasn't our cup of tea, and we couldn't get that either. On empty stomachs, we headed off anyway. After getting lost on our way to Ginza, we surveyed the map of Tokyo for the tenth time and realized that we were heading the wrong way.

The first challenge you will encounter is that there are no street numbers in Tokyo. How is Tokyo going to handle the Olympics? Alas, a Starbucks! A real latte was just the ticket to replenish our batteries, and the employees spoke English, a rare treat as we were realizing. We checked the map for the eleventh time. Tokyo Tower must be around here somewhere, we thought. We looked up and realized that the shadows protecting us from the hot sun were in fact the Tokyo Tower. We

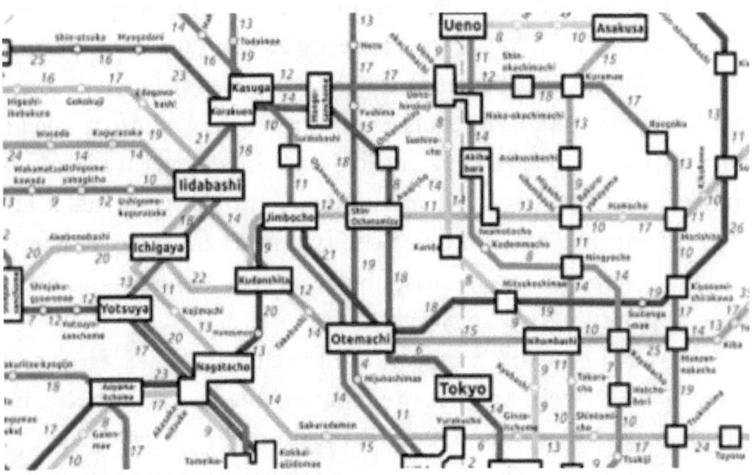

SPAGHETTI TRAIN ROUTE MAP

headed for the Imperial Palace, the permanent residence of Japan's Emperor and Imperial family. The Palace itself is a contemporary reconstruction of the Meiji Imperial Palace, which was targeted by aerial bombers during World War 2. What was amazing was that this structure surrounded by magnificent, expertly trimmed trees, pristine lawns, and a beautiful crystal clear lake was in the middle of a concrete jungle known as Tokyo. A pine-like smell filled the air.

Off to Tokyo station now, where we purchased our Pasmo cards, which enabled us to travel on all the spaghetti-linked lines of the Tokyo underground. Our advice was good because some passes only allow travel on certain lines, and that would have made it even more confusing than it already was.

The Yamanote line to Yurakucho station was where we headed next. The underground system was like another city. People everywhere, not missing stride even when you were taking their path. It seemed to work. No head-on crashes. Best of all, the announcements on the train were in Japanese and English and they even told you what side of the train to get off. Wow. Yakitori Alley. Narrow alleyways under the train line.

Traditional lanterns lit up each restaurant. It seemed as if the Tokyo government had forgotten about the people under the subway line when they modernised the city. And thankfully, they had. Each restaurant had four tables at most, accompanied by little square stools, that weren't that comfortable at best. However, it didn't matter. This was how I pictured Tokyo in the '60s. Choices on the menu were limited. Deep fried scallops, noodles to remind us of the spaghetti train system, and oysters. That was it. One dish, but this was a blessing as they didn't speak English anyway.

A traditional soft drink would have been nice. Sprite? No. Juice? No. Oh well. At least the Japanese tea was quite refreshing. It was 1840 yen or $19 AUD for lunch for three.

We took a return trip on the spaghetti train system to our

stop at Shimbashi. Pasmos are fantastic. That night we tried a taxi, at 487 yen or $5 to the Tsukiji Central Fish Market. Acres and acres of fish. They say that if you get there at 4

PASMO CARD FOR TRAIN TRAVEL

am, you have to take a ticket to get in and even then entry isn't guaranteed due to the large numbers. But hey! We are on holiday, so 6 pm will do us. Much of the market was closed by then, and traders had pulled down their shutters to get ready for another early start. The smell of fish filled the air, but strangely enough, it was a fresh fish smell.

TOKYO FISH MARKET

A smattering of little restaurants were scattered along the laneways; they were offering fresh sashimi and sushi—and wasn't it fresh! We chose a restaurant that looked good and as we entered everyone cheered, including other guests. We couldn't understand how they knew we were Australian, only to find out that they did it for everyone, and what an atmosphere it created. The sushi selection was to die for, as was its freshness. It melted in your mouth. It was 2,224 yen or $23 AUD for dinner including Coke and Japanese tea. Still no Sprite and no English, but who cared? This was exceptional. Surely, we couldn't do Tokyo on $100 per day for three people?

TOP: TYPICAL RESTAURANT
BOTTOM: TEMPLE

Off to Disneyland next, Tokyo style. We caught the train to Disneyland, and we only got lost once. We were getting the gist of the spaghetti system. Interestingly, we had entered the underground from our hotel foyer, then walked against the traffic of businesspeople on their way to work, dodging and weaving and weaving and dodging. I had never seen so many people at any one time in one place, and all were on the move. We had breakfast in one of the cafes in this underground metropolis, spent around an hour underground from when we left the hotel, and when we arrived at Disneyland and came up for air, only then did we realize it had been raining.

We could see Cinderella's Castle and the Disneyland Hotel because both towered over the park, which is slightly smaller than Anaheim. We walked through the entrance, walked through Cinderella's Castle, and straight to Fantasyland. We went on the carousel and then to Snow White's Adventures on a carriage, which takes you through the ride featuring moving ornaments and scenery. We saw Peter Pan's Flight, a Small World, and the Haunted Mansion with a running commentary in Japanese, so we had no idea how scary it was.

The ultimate after beginning to miss European meals was Alice's Tea Party, where we ate burgers and nuggets shaped like Mickey Mouse. Was I really doing this? This is Tokyo.

Toon Town, Adventure Land, and The Pirates of the Caribbean ride. The Pirates all looked very real and this was before our first drink. Tomorrowland and then the Star Jets. Disneyland is a must-see. Even without children. It might bring the child back in you.

We got back on the train and headed back to Shimbashi

TARA WITH DONALD DUCK   HAUNTED MANSION

station, only having to change lines twice. That night we took a brisk ten-minute walk through the underground city and chose a quaint little Chinese restaurant for dinner, one of many on offer in this strange new concept of living.

It was $23 for dinner including drinks. Yes, you guessed it. Japanese tea and Coke. Still no Sprite or English. Thank god though for the pictures on the menu.

This underground spaghetti system not only offers an extremely efficient transport system servicing around three million commuters each day once you get used to it, but it also offers an extensive and cost-effective way to eat fresh and varied food in a spotless environment. It is like another city, except that it is underground.

The next morning, we had breakfast again at the Shimbashi underground. They still don't speak English, but they are starting to recognize us. How could they not? French toast and a real latte, but sugar syrup, which I wasn't game to try. Again only around $16 for breakfast. I found out later that when I went off to find a chemist, Kerri and Tara had to queue to get in, as it was full. The manager saw them at the door and moved four people to make way for them. That is the Japanese for you.

Onto the Ueno line now heading for Asakusa. Charming little streets, only to be outdone by charming little shops. I could stay here forever. Our first venture was to the historic Shitamachi district and the Senso-ji Temple.

Old world streets, little shopping arcades, and lunch in a side street cafe that only sat about six people. No English, but great pictures on the menu, again a lifesaver for those who don't speak Japanese. The service and keen intent to help were amazing. Still, no Sprite, but a bill for $18 helped our disappointment. After seeing some magnificent shrines, some of them dating back to the seventh century, we headed by foot to Higashi Hongan, home to over 300 temples. Then as we crossed into Kappabashi Dori, we came across shop upon shop selling plastic food models.

We later realized that just about every restaurant in Tokyo must use these models to display their featured dishes in the windows of their premises. And they look real! Well, almost anyway. We reluctantly headed back on the Ginza line train to Ueno and walked around the Ameyoko Arcade, another quaint little open-air arcade of shops nestled amongst the shrines, temples, and multi-story apartment blocks. Planning will not necessarily deliver you all of this. You need to be prepared to wander, and you will discover and discover and continually discover.

We took the bullet train (Shinkansen) off to Kyoto, although it wasn't that easy. Our vouchers for travel processed in Australia had to be redeemed. However, after travelling from platform to platform and service desk to service desk throughout Tokyo station, it became apparent that Tokyo's train system is run by multiple non-related companies. The distinctive lack of English-speaking personnel was beginning to become frustrating.

What was more frustrating was that while I was standing on the left-hand side of the escalator with my daughter and our luggage, my wife flew past on the right-hand side, because she had found herself in the express lane by mistake. The pure number of people on the escalator, and the almost obedient culture, meant that your destiny was controlled by the crowds. We found her a few days later.

Kyoto was incredible. Another step back in time, and as we soon found out, the previous capital of Japan up until the mid-1800s. We had lunch at a little place on Main Street down from the Westin Miyako, which mirrored the great modern hotels of Singapore and Dubai. Luckily, I had checked my socks that morning for holes as we had to take off our shoes as we entered. The biggest challenge was having to sit cross-legged along the table. Or was it having to get up after lunch?

That night, we waited for our tour bus, but when it ran

over fifteen minutes late, we investigated and found that the company had changed the pickup destination. Remember, nothing runs late in Japan. We quickly got a taxi to another destination point, and joined the tour group, just in time. Multiple taxis took us to a restaurant where again our shoes were removed, but this time there was room under the table so we didn't need to cross our legs.

There are only seventeen geishas training in Kyoto out of a population of over 1,500,000. One of them, dressed in a beautiful kimono, with traditional makeup and hair, entered the room and danced to a medley of traditional songs. She didn't speak English, but an interpreter answered many questions for us. Chosen at fifteen years of age, and now seventeen, she would have to decide in three years, if she passed, whether this would be her destiny, dedicated to Old Japanese tradition.

In the morning, we joined another tour that started with the Nijo castle. Off came the shoes again.

The floor squeaked as we walked, resembling birds chirping. This was constructed so that the Shogun warriors and the

MT. FUJI AND LAKE KAWAGUCHIKO

Emperor could hear if ninjas had entered through the darkness of night. This holy shrine was rebuilt in the sixteenth century after being hit by lightning.

Our next stop, the Golden Pavilion, was a highlight as it is actually made out of gold that reflects off the surrounding moats, with beautifully sculptured trees and rock gardens. Our trip back wasn't without incident, as again we couldn't redeem our travel vouchers. Our MasterCard was taking a hit at $405 each way.

On our return, we decided to change at a few lines and get off at Harajuku. This is Tokyo's famous fashion bazaar, and it really is bizarre. Not only does the YouTube video of people being squashed onto trains not do this stop justice, but there was little more room when you entered Takeshita Dori. Side shops, stores, people dressed in weird outfits; an amusement arcade that held more people than Wembley, Madison Square Garden, or the MCG, and was mainly attended by over forty-year-old males. Every teenager in Tokyo had to be on this one street that was so narrow that a car couldn't have travelled through it without the crowds even if it wanted to.

The train ride out of there was a little more civilised, that was until we got off at Shibuya station and headed to the world-famous Shibuya crossing. People everywhere. A rave party would have nothing on this. Wall-to-wall shops. Fashion, food, and then again some. This is the Tokyo you see on TV. The neon lights and one store had twelve floors of fashion alone. We had to have McDonald's for dinner that evening, just so that we could come back to reality.

After being picked up at the hotel next to where we were staying, we boarded the bus for a two-hour trip to Mount Fuji. As we neared, we saw in the distance this unbelievable mound dwarfing all other mountains around. The clouds covered the peak that stood nearly 4,000 metres above sea level. By the time we had reached the fifth station, 2,700 metres above sea level, the clouds had cleared, and it was a surreal feeling to look up to the summit, which could only be reached on foot, and by experienced and very fit climbers to say the least. In fact, the clouds had formed below us, giving us the feeling that we were travelling in a plane above the clouds.

After spending an hour taking photos, we proceeded for lunch and headed down the mountain to the gondola. Accommodating a party of eight, the gondola took us back up the mountain, climbing above the trees and vegetation below us to where we were met once again by the bus and travelled to the active volcanic region of Hakone.

SHIBUYA

An awkward stench filled the air, as the sulphur, mixed with volcanic particles, spat up out of the ground. It reminded you of opening a packet of eggs that had gone way past the use-by date. Entrepreneurs have turned this into a lucrative money spinner on the mountain, as when eggs are boiled in the springs, they become black. Eating one is said to add seven years to your life. You may eat up to two and a half to add up to seventeen and a half years extra to your life, but eating a whole third is said to give you a belly ache and time in the hospital.

Oh, did I forget to mention that the black ice cream tasted of egg? Our final tour was to the pristine Lake Hakone, where we boarded a tall ship, and sailed the lake for thirty minutes. A return trip on the Shinkansen had us back to Tokyo in no time.

KYOTO STREET

Our final day saw us travelling back to Tokyo in the '60s, or that is what it seemed like. Hanazono on the Marunouchi line heading towards Shinjuku is such a place. Little streets, fashion from the '60s, and signs that were made closer to post-war than post-Internet.

Laneways winding down the hill are filled with cobblestones where a single lane of traffic has to make way for pedestrians walking to the shopping centre to get their daily groceries. This final day capped off the incredible experience that Tokyo is.

It's not just the high-rise concrete jungle of tomorrow. It's the electronic leader of the world. The manufacturers of the best-selling motor vehicles in Australia. In complete contrast. A proud tradition. A proud and almost mechanical population providing a safe environment where Westerners are almost idolised and the American influences are testimony to that. A will to please and assist on every occasion and remarkably, with the right advice, it can be experienced for under $100 a day.

My five favourite activities to cover in Tokyo

(Very difficult to limit it to five, so I didn't.)

1. The Ginza Tokyo
2. Yakitori Alley
3. Asakusa
4. Hanazono
5. Harajuku
5.5 Kyoto

SAIGON (Ho Chi Minh), VIETNAM

My advice: expect the unexpected.

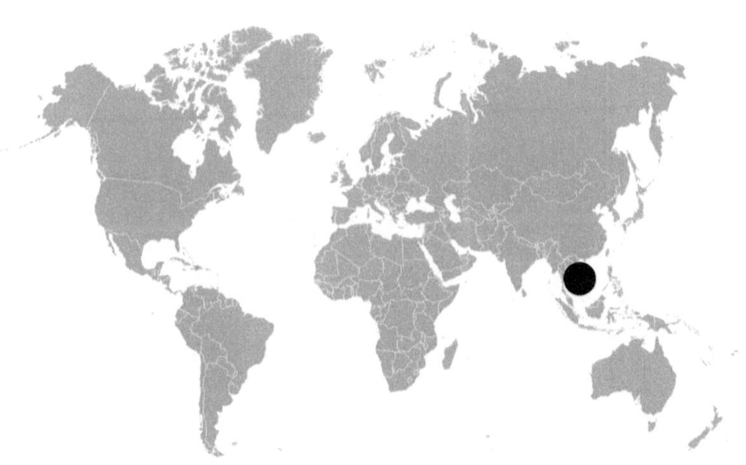

Ho Chi Minh City (*Thành phố Hồ Chí Minh*), commonly known to the locals as Saigon, especially if you want them to respond to you, has the largest population of any city in Vietnam. Most of the locals are still not accepting of the change of government to the North Vietnamese, and hence still refer to their territory as Saigon.

The city consists of twenty-four districts; District One is regarded as city central, and is home to many of the higher-end chains of hotels. It is also the financial hub of Vietnam.

The architecture of Saigon, and Hanoi for that matter, was strongly influenced by the French. Many of the old buildings still strike a resemblance to French architecture from the nineteenth century. Many are testament to the early ties that Vietnam shared with the French. Today, however, much of the new development is influenced by modernist contemporary designs highlighting the country's own Vietnamese unique identity

I was employed by a company in 2016 whose managing director was living in Vietnam, to launch a new manufacturing plant just outside of Ho Chi Minh City.

I was extremely interested in experiencing for myself the intricacies involved in establishing a new plant, but also I am the first to admit that I wanted to obtain a sense of appreciation and establish some visibility as not just another employee in the company. Plus, I could claim tax on the trip.

I started the process. I googled "Learn Vietnamese" and commenced to work with a Vietnamese lady at her home. I started to feel a real infinity with the language, especially as she commented that I had a natural gift of using my voice to deliver the correct pronunciation. Vietnamese, like German or Spanish, use diacritics, often loosely called accents, to affect their pronunciation and in some cases meanings. Some examples are as follows:

ma means but
ma means mother
ma means ghost

So, you can see the danger of mispronouncing the word by not inflecting your voice correctly to match the diacritic.

Expect the unexpected

I arrived in Vietnam around mid-morning and caught a taxi to my hotel in District One. The atmosphere was just as I imagined it would be. Bicycles everywhere, motorcycles tooting the cars, and cars tooting the motorcycles. I learned later that we Westerners toot our horn when someone pisses us off, but in Vietnam, it is to warn them that they are there, before they piss you off.

As we are driving, I am looking out the window, like a young boy who first enters a sweet shop. It's crazy. One motorbike pulls next to the taxi, with a mother driving with a maybe two-year-old on her lap, and a six-year-old on the back holding on for dear life. The lights change from red to green and off she goes, luckily with all baggage intact. Another passes, with a bar fridge tied to the seat of the motorcycle, and the driver positioned precariously on the back.

We arrived at the hotel without incident, and I settled in for an afternoon of exploring, within a safe distance of the hotel, just in case I got lost.

Lunch was my favourite. Grilled pork with vermicelli noodles and nuts on top.

As I was walking up the main street, I caught something out of the corner of my eye. Just as I focused, my gold chain was ripped from my neck, and the motorcyclist, who had driven up onto the footpath, took off like grease lightning. I chased to no avail, which is just as well. If I had caught him, I would've been charged with murder.

I was a little stunned, but more so angry, that I could let this happen. Why didn't I see him earlier? I went into a beauty parlour and asked them to call the police.

Unfortunately, they didn't speak English, and the lady who taught me Vietnamese hadn't taught me how to say 'police.'

I returned to the hotel with my tail between my legs. I reported it to reception, who asked me to fill out a form. At least I could claim insurance and I had proof of it being stolen. From then on, my vision was at 360 degrees wherever I walked.

My neck must have been jolted when he pulled the chain because it was quite sore. You know the feeling, when you are somewhere and for some reason, you turn quickly, and a spasm hits your neck, and you are paralyzed until you get up enough guts to move it, and then it is fine.

Across the road from the hotel, I saw a massage shop that looked legitimate, as it also included a beauty shop specializing in nails and hair. I entered and was ushered upstairs. The girl spoke no English, but I was able to communicate to her my issue, and after about thirty minutes of rubbing and some liniment, I was feeling better. It was only my ego that was still hurting from my incident.

I awoke early and had a nice breakfast in the hotel. The toots had started early, so I popped down to the Sheraton, which had a nice coffee shop out the front, yet could still service the guests of the Sheraton at the rear.

It was starting to heat up, and the humidity was unbearable. It was only 8 am. A few street vendors walked past offering cold drinks in makeshift Eskys, handing out bottles of water to entice a purchase. Interestingly, the next day it poured while I was sitting in the same spot, and the same vendors walked past, selling umbrellas and ponchos. Talk about reading the market.

I was keen to explore the Ben Thanh market, which I was told was one of the best markets in Vietnam. I not only love a bargain, but I love the hustle and bustle of a market, its eccentric shop owners, varied produce, and not-so-varied produce.

Just then a man riding a bicycle with a cart attached approached me, asking if I wanted a ride. Cycle rickshaws are known as xích lô (pronounced sick-low, from the French cyclo) in Vietnam.

Naively, I replied "Can you take me to Ben Thanh market?" Of course, he said yes.

I asked how much and he replied with $10 AUD, somehow identifying me as Australian.

We seemed to go for hours. Riding around roundabouts, with cars heading straight for us, and me in the front seat, wondering if my travel insurance would cover being hit by a car.

I could swear that Ben Thanh market wasn't this far away.

All of a sudden, he stopped outside a house and left the bicycle and me sitting inside the cart. He knocked on the door, and two ladies appeared, one in her nightgown, and the other in a miniskirt that barely covered her neck. Both appeared half asleep. He turned to me and said, "You want lady." I emphatically said no, much to the disgust of the two ladies standing there. I demanded he take me to Ben Thanh market, but he repeated his initial request, so I got out of the cart and started walking.

I had no idea where I was, or how I was going to get back to the hotel, but all I knew was that I was not going to hang around. I walked for about thirty minutes, not even sure that I was walking in the right direction. I saw a taxi at a petrol station and asked if he could take me to my hotel. It cost around

160,000 Vietnamese dong, about $10, and we were only about five minutes from the hotel.

If this was my first few days in Vietnam, I wanted to go home. I called my wife and told her so.

INTERIOR BEN THANH MARKET

The following day, after a good night's sleep, I reflected on my earlier experiences and realized that it was naivety that had gotten me into those situations. I headed off to Ben Thanh market with instructions and a map from the hotel staff. I was hoping this market was going to be worth it. And it was. An abundance of clothing, from T-shirts to underwear, to electrical goods, to dress-making materials. It had everything. I tried to listen in on conversations, to try and understand what they were saying. After all, I had over six months of lessons. I understood absolutely nothing.

They were speaking so quickly that by the time I understood one word, or thought I did, they had moved on. I felt it would be easier if I spoke in Vietnamese; that way, not only could they see I was trying, but also I could do it at my pace. Forget it. Just use Google.

I started heading back to the hotel, because its location

was very central, and it was extremely uncomfortable in the heat, although I did love it. My neck started hurting again, so on my return, I remembered the massage shop, where the girl had really strong hands and had relieved some of my pain.

She was there again, and I think remembered me and began to work on my neck. Again at the end of the thirty minutes, it felt so much better, and I wanted to thank her sincerely for her efforts.

I became quite friendly with this girl and her boss, and one day, they invited me over for chicken at lunchtime in the salon. To reciprocate, I invited them both for dinner at my hotel, as the restaurant was on top of the building, and looked out over District One.

I met them as they entered the foyer, and started heading towards the lift. All of a sudden, security sprung from everywhere, shouting in Vietnamese. Eventually, they both went to the reception desk and handed them their licenses, which the desk held onto until they left.

I found out later from one of the porters that the hotel has very strict ethical rules, and no single women are allowed

HUSTLE AND BUSTLE OF SAIGON STREET

to enter the hotel, even as guests of a guest. Also, it is to protect their guests, like me, from anything untoward happening to them. Finally, a Western man and a local woman cannot be together in the hotel rooms unless they are married.

I understood all of that, but all we were doing was going to their restaurant on the top floor for dinner. I was pleased, however, that I was staying at a very ethical hotel.

Just before I departed for Vietnam, quite a few staff were retrenched from the business. These things happen, I understand. However, what I couldn't accept was why it was done so close to Christmas. I know two of the women had young families and were devasted; I could see their concerns about going through the holiday period with financial constraints.

I was picked up in a chauffeur-driven vehicle by the boss, and we headed to the new plant, just outside of Saigon. It was a forty-minute drive, which gave us plenty of time to get to know each other and to talk about sales projections for the next calendar year, and the challenges we were facing.

At that stage, I thought that this was a good career move, and what better way to establish myself within the business than to have a one-on-one with the boss. As we came around a corner, the boss commented that he wanted to buy the empty land sitting between two warehouses, as well as two warehouses, as he thought they would be good investments. So much so that he had already put in offers. Wait a minute—you have retrenched three people before Christmas with families, and yet you are going out spending money like it is going out of fashion? I am afraid my ethics don't agree with this. Anyway, I needn't have worried. I was retrenched one year later.

My wife, Kerri, joined me on my next trip, and because of familiarity, we stayed at the same hotel in District One. I took her to my old haunts, like Ben Thanh market and the restaurant where I devoured my serving of grilled pork and vermicelli noodles.

We also met up with my girl masseuse and her chaperone, the boss, but couldn't eat until the salon closed at 10 pm. It was a real experience to not only eat at that time but to see how many others were eating at that time. The place was packed to the rafters. I decided to walk back to the hotel, but Kerri took a taxi. Kerri is a very strong-willed person; she picks up spiders and puts them outside. Nothing much fazes her. Except cockroaches, and on her way back to the hotel, a cockroach crawled up her leg while in the taxi. The poor taxi driver, who didn't speak English, had no idea what Kerri was saying, only that she was screaming, and jumping all around the back seat of the taxi. She made the driver stop, and she got out while the taxi driver searched for, found, and removed the cockroach. When I finally arrived back at the hotel, she was a wreck.

We did have a great time though, and even though I returned another time on my own, and visited the resort town of Nha Trang, it was certainly more pleasurable to share the experiences rather than being on my own.

We organized a tour down the Mekong River, although most of the action does occur at 4 am, so we did find our late morning visit a little blasé.

I taught Kerri to cross the road in District One. It is, however, the same as in all the other districts. Close your eyes and walk. They will miss you, I was told. Don't hesitate or look at who or what is heading towards you. That's when you will get into trouble.

We visited the war museum, which I must mention was heavily North Vietnamese influenced. It depicted a war that shouldn't have happened, nor should the sentiment of how those involved were treated on their return. However, whilst the tour was incredible, and you were able to identify the areas of communist influence, your eyes were certainly opened. Unfortunately, I had to walk out at one stage, when the subject of Agent Orange was covered with images, and sit on my own outside, to regather my composure.

Another option in Saigon is to tour and explore the tunnels of Cu Chi, which were used by the Viet Cong during the Vietnam War to provide protection, launch surprise attacks, or just travel underground for up to 120 km, without being detected. I believe they are very small and perhaps overweight people may struggle. However, because I am claustrophobic, I will never know, because I will never try.

You can't go to Vietnam without experiencing all the delights that the street food has to offer. The aromatic flavours and the individual textures, when mixed, offer a unique blend of tastes, often never experienced before.

We walked down Bui Vien Street just before dark, and the redolent scents just hit you as you neared a street food stall. It was difficult to identify the source, as all the aromas seemed to blend into one aroma.

A small tea candle kept the Pho warm, but you wondered how. However, Pho at 30,000 VND was too good to bypass. Kerri decided to order Bun Xio (a variation on rice cakes), which we decided to share. Total cost 105,000 VND ($6 AUD)

The following night, even though we were tempted to order the same dishes as the night before, we found a van, with signs on the side, advertising Bun Cha (a grilled pork and noodle dish) which I couldn't resist. 128,000 VND or $8 AUD. Kerri wasn't in the mood for pork, and was a little worried about eating pork from a street vendor (she can have a delicate tummy), so she ordered xoi, which is a kind of sticky rice. Again, the prices were ridiculous.

The next evening, we went down one of the side streets, off Bui Vien Street. Up until now, we hadn't seen one of our favourites, banh mi.

We went up to a small café with its menu stuck on the front window.

Bahn mi for 10,000 VND. We went in to order and even though the interior decorator had missed this place, it appeared clean, and you could see the chef cooking through an open window, which is always a good sign, and the kitchen looked respectable also.

We ordered two banh mi, but the lady with quite good English suggested we order goi cuon, a prawn and rice dish mixed with vermicelli noodles and wrapped in a rice paper roll. The drinks we ordered were dearer than the meals, but both dishes, which we shared, were sensational.

I did have a little upset stomach the next day, but that could've been from anything.

SAIGON CITY HALL, HO CHI MINH CITY

I mentioned before that I spent a week in Nha Trang. It is a quaint seaside resort, with a sensational night market, and a large variety of smaller family- owned shops spread throughout the town.

I walked past a jewelry store, which was like a gold warehouse. My chain that had been stolen in Saigon was insured for $1,200 AUD, so I telephoned my wife, and discussed whether it was worth buying another one from here. (Actually, it was more like begging my wife.)

The girl showed me a finely linked gold chain, completely

different from the one I had stolen. Yet it was appealing, maybe because it would be more discreet around my neck. She asked my nationality and quoted me $200 AUD. I thanked her but decided to walk it off and think about whether or not I should buy it. I went for lunch and made up my mind that I liked it, and $200 was a very reasonable price.

I returned to the store, and the girl recognized me immediately; I told her that I would purchase the chain. I handed her my credit card and she went to the computer to register the purchase. She returned, advising me that the price of gold had just dropped and it was now only $170 AUD. What? Talk about ethics and honesty. Anyway, to this day, I still wear it with pride.

Vietnam is fast becoming a tourist hot spot, simply because of its diverse culture, influenced by the French, and now run by a communist government, although half the country failed to accept the new regime.

It boasts places such as Hanoi, the most northern city in Vietnam, Halong Bay, filled with beautiful and picturesque scenery, and Da Nang, surrounded by mountains, the Han River, and the East Sea. Vietnam has so much to offer.

My five must sees and dos in Saigon

1. Ben Thanh Market
2. Cu Chi Tunnels
3. Mekong Delta
4. War Remnants Museum
5. Street Food Tour

NOUMEA, NEW CALEDONIA

My advice: expect the unexpected.

I am the first to admit that Nouméa was not very high on my bucket list. In fact, it wasn't there at all. However, we needed to get away on a holiday to celebrate our anniversary and Noumea, on the face of it, appeared cheap. The airfares and accommodation were very reasonable.

When you mention to most that you are going to Nouméa, people usually respond with a puzzled look. After all, most visit Nouméa by ship, as a one-night stopover on their cruise to greener pastures or bluer seas. Of course, all they see is the city and Nouméa's CBD (Central Business District), which not only lacks ambience, it lacks most things, except homeless, dirty alleyways, rubbish in streets, and vacant for lease signs on every second shop.

However, all is not lost, as those in the know remember

ANSE VATA BEACH

the old Club Med Nouméa and unfortunately, the stopovers don't allow you enough time to visit the extreme opposite of Nouméa's CBD.

After some relatively brief research, we found the resort had been taken over by the Chateau Royal and after a quick visit to Webjet, were convinced that this was the solution we were looking for, as it indeed ticked all the boxes, especially the white sandy beaches with pristine water. And the price.

Nouméa, here we come.

Qantas Airways flies to Nouméa; however, they generally have one stopover, meaning the flying time is extended out to five hours. Every negative turns into a positive, because most flights take off in the afternoon, and the airports are so quiet that check-in, security, and toilet stops become a breeze.

I love the French, and over thirty years ago, I learned to speak French through cassettes. I grasped the language so well that I could actually speak 100 words fluently. Well, almost fluently. Maybe not quite fluently. Anyway, Nouméa was the closest region with French influences, so we travelled to Nouméa so that I could practice. Unfortunately, most spoke English.

However, I digress. Thirty years on, we return with expectations relatively low, but thankfully our expenses are just as low.

We arrived at 6 pm; it was already very dark, and a few raindrops let off a sweet scent when mixed with the humidity. It was April, which is the end of the rainy season.

As we looked for our car rental (the resort is one hour from the airport, and located near Anse Vata Beach), all signage was in French. Where were these signs thirty years ago? My daughter, Tara, had learned French at school, so she was able to figure out what direction we should head to collect our car.

Having achieved our first goal, we could see our little (cheap) hire car waiting for us. I had ordered a Peugeot manual over an automatic, purely because of the price. Even though I hadn't driven a manual for over forty years, I wasn't fazed. That was until we got in the car. I had forgotten that they drive on the other side of the road, so not only do I have to focus on putting my foot on the clutch and changing gears with my hands, I now have to do it with my right hand. Rule one: research. Rule two: see rule one.

My wife, Kerri, suggested we drive around the car park so I could familiarize myself with the manual transmission, the left-hand drive, and the complete darkness from very limited street lighting. No. I was confident. I immediately put it into first, drove straight over the nature strip, and after barely missing a light pole that was useless anyway, we hit the highway.

Not wanting to be recognized as a visiting driver, we sat at the speed limit of seventy miles per hour. Whilst I was handling the gears well, it was a challenge because of the poor street lighting and the fact that the rain was getting heavier and heavier. I asked Kerri to open the glove box to retrieve a map or a NAVMAN, so that we could find our way to Anse Vata Beach, approximately fifteen minutes past the city. Neither was in the glove box. How were we going to find our way there? Oh well, we decided that with signs to the city, we could always ask someone for further directions. Hopefully in English. We had been travelling at seventy miles an hour for about thirty minutes, when Tara, from the back seat, noticed a man in a truck making gestures to her. She couldn't work out what they meant. Finger to thumb, finger to thumb. OMG. I had been driving with no lights on.

To everyone's amazement, including my own, we reached our destination, well within the estimated time as noted in the hotel pamphlets. Setting aside my careful driving and expert judgment, my wife pretty much opened the passenger door, stumbled out, and burst into tears. The concept of driving on the wrong side of the road at seventy miles per hour in the rain, with no lights on, was just too much for her. We put our bags in the room and went straight to the hotel's dining room for a well-earned meal. After dinner on returning to our apartment, we were really pleased. It appeared that the hotel had combined two apartments, each with one bedroom. Tara's room was at one end, followed by a corridor leading to a self-contained kitchen on one side, and a beautiful lounge room with exquisite fixtures and fittings, followed by the extension of the corridor leading to our bedroom. Concertina doors gave us some privacy.

The next morning, we woke to our first day in paradise. We opened the blinds covering the balcony and blocking our view of the beach. It was unbelievable. If we could've afforded it, we would have paid more. Looking down, we could see a beautiful pool surrounded by lush vegetation, leading onto the beach with crystal clear waters. They were so clear, it felt like you were looking down onto a mirror from six storeys up. This is what we dreamed of. A dip in the pool, then ten steps

VIEW FROM HOTEL ROOM ONTO ANSE VATA BEACH

to our private beach, and a swim in pristine Pacific waters. And yes, this is where we spent our first day. It was priceless.

That evening, we walked about fifty metres from the hotel into the shopping area filled with outdoor restaurants and cafes. After much discussion, Italian became our unanimous choice. We ordered two Carbonara and one Napoli. Three soft drinks, but no dessert. 1200 francs. $300 AUD. OMG. This holiday was supposed to be on the cheap.

Another day of lounging by the pool and swimming at the beach was followed by an evening meal at the Sushi Train, one of Tara's favourite restaurants. Of course, we assumed that it would be a lot less expensive than the night before. 710 francs or $180 AUD. My god, this place is expensive. Still, the negatives tend to disappear into oblivion when your only worry is to swim in the pool or the Pacific Ocean.

At around 5 am the following morning, we awoke to the sound of a helicopter that felt so close, we thought it had landed on our balcony. Opening our blinds, we had to adjust our eyes to the bright sunlight coming off the water, and the thoughts of yet another day in paradise doing nothing, except lying on the beach.

We could see a helicopter hovering what seemed like only metres from the water. They appeared to be searching for something, although it's not unusual for emergency services to be practicing maneuvers in safety simulations.

Today's agenda hadn't changed. In fact, it replicated yesterday and the day before. Down to the pool for a wake-up dip, lie on the beach to relax, and swim in the ocean. Firstly, however, it was time for breakfast. We headed down to the restaurant overlooking the pool and out to the Pacific Ocean.

I stopped at reception and queried the activity of the helicopter.

Unfortunately, the receptionist stated, two taxi boats had collided during the evening while heading out to a party on one of the islands. Two people were dead and one was missing. She added that the beach was now closed as it was a crime scene.

Very sad indeed. Selfishly, we were disappointed that the beach was closed, as it was one of the major reasons for our decision to come to Nouméa. But this was not the time to be selfish. How awful for the family and the wider New Caledonian community.

As we embarked on our daily walk to Anse Vata shopping strip for fresh croissants and jam, around ten locals were sitting on the hill looking out to the ocean, crying and hoping that good news would follow. Their vigil lasted for the rest of our holiday.

Shaken, we learned to accept their distress, and smiled at the group as we passed every day.

That night, we headed out for dinner. Out of the corner of my eye, I saw a sandwich board in the hotel foyer, advising that a cyclone category one was on its way and scheduled to hit within days.

The following morning, a maintenance team knocked on our door and commenced relocating the outdoor furniture from the balcony to our lounge room. They then proceeded to stick masking tape on all of our windows. Was this happening?

We realized the seriousness of this weather event when we headed out for dinner, only to find that many of the restaurants had pulled their shutters down in preparation, and closed indefinitely or until it was safe to reopen.

The following morning, we noticed that the sandwich board had been updated to advise that the cyclone had been upgraded to a category two, and no one was allowed out of the hotel. A memo delivered to every room advised that microwave meals could be purchased from reception until the cyclone had passed.

The cyclone hit around 1 am, and it was an eerie feeling. Pitch black with slight silhouettes of the trees appearing from ground lighting, as all other lighting was non-existent. The trees were permanently tilted to one side, almost like a competition amongst the trees as to which one could touch the ground without loosening its roots.

My microwave meal was coq au vin, which is a well-known French chicken stew where pieces of meat are braised in a luscious, glossy red wine sauce with bacon, mushroom, and onions. Supposedly. What an adventure, sitting in the loungeroom with our blinds open, eating a microwave meal whilst watching the palm trees starting to sway horizontally. There are many things to do in Noumea. If you want to explore, there is much to see and enjoy.

By morning, as the hot sun poked through the clouds, the aftermath was evident for all to see. Palm tree fronds (leaves) covered the ground. The crystal-clear waters of the pool were filled with branches of every kind floating as if they had found a new home. And to add to the devastation, Kerri had food

EXPERIENCING CYCLONE

poisoning, or gastro, all at the same time, and she had admitted the night before that her bouillabaisse was quite tasty and tender. Of course, she missed all of the excitement. She was either asleep or in the toilet, bringing up the day's takings.

The council workers were out in the streets, with their makeshift brooms, and trucks driving past were filled with thousands and thousands of palm tree fronds. The clear waters of the Pacific had turned grey, with bits of bark, silt from the bottom of the ocean floor, and other rubbish being dragged by the currents.

I had booked a surprise romantic dinner for our anniversary at a restaurant that was situated at the end of the pier, where you could view the fish swimming peacefully under your feet while eating barramundi. The restaurant was closed 'until further notice,' and it made you wonder how the fish would cope with the impending rough seas.

Top five things to do and must-sees

1. The Island Turtle Tour

    This tour of Signal Island is a must. We experienced the turtle adventure in Hawaii and it really makes you feel that you are in the cast of *Finding Nemo*.

2. The Amedee Lighthouse

    The lighthouse is beautiful, but so too is the opportunity to embark on a glass-bottomed boat tour. The lighthouse is always within distance and soars over fifty metres above the small island that accommodates it. The lighthouse was actually constructed in Paris.

3. Tjibaou Cultural Centre

It is worth taking a guided tour, accessible from the cruise terminal, to appreciate the dedication to local art. The French influences come to the fore, especially when visiting the church within the grounds.

4. Anse Vata Beach

We have spoken of our Anse Vata experiences, but apart from all the issues out of our control, this is an amazing part of the world. It is one of the main tourist spots in New Calédonia, with beaches covered in soft white sands, and waters glistening from the sun watching over from above.

We never saw the families of the missing person again, nor did we hear if they had been found. It doesn't matter how much you plan, there are some things you can't control.

****It must be noted that in May 2024, the French Government passed a law allowing residents who have lived in the territory for at least ten years the right to vote in provincial elections. Some local leaders fear this will dilute the vote of the indigenous Kanak.

Riots have broken out, with cars burnt out and blocking highways. As a result, the airport has been closed. One thousand French troops have been sent to Noumea to try and restore law and order.

BYRON BAY, NEW SOUTH WALES, AUSTRALIA

My advice: expect the unexpected.

Byron Bay is home to many famous people such as Zac Efron, Chris Hemsworth, Matt Damon, Elsa Pataky, Tim Cahill, and Elyse Knowles.

The reason they live here is quite simple: they can afford it. Real estate prices are high, but so are the stunning views and the unique cultural atmosphere.

The city is also known for its laid-back lifestyle, which is another reason why it's a desirable place to live. Coming from a conservative background, it was initially challenging for me to adapt to Byron Bay's culture and cuisine.

However, I decided to embrace the challenge and did some research to find the perfect accommodation. I chose to stay at Elements on Byron, a new resort built on a twenty-hectare site at Belongil Beach, which is about four km away from the city centre.

The resort has 170 villas, which are a mix of one- and two-bedroom units, equipped with all the modern amenities one would expect.

The developer's managing director, Peggy Flannery, purchased the site for $18.5m in 2009. The resort features two kilometres of beachfront, a reserve of coastal rainforest, and natural lakes and ponds. It is a unique and wonderful destination that would even satisfy those who are hard to please.

On our first evening, the heavens opened up. The constant rain pelted down, as it can in Northern NSW, onto our eco-constructed tin roof. I slept like a log because nothing soothes me more than rain on a hot tin roof.

In the morning, we all gathered for breakfast and started discussing our plans for the day. Certainly, as the rain was still quite heavy, lying at the beach sunbaking and swimming in

BYRON BAY BEACH

the ocean was probably out.

I suggested Nimbin. Nimbin is known the world over as Australia's most famous hippie destination and alternative lifestyle capital and is only a one-hour or so drive from Byron Bay unless you take the scenic route.

We all agreed, grabbed our mobile phones and fashion accessories, and headed to the car.

It was still raining, so we had our rain jackets on, and as we got to the car, I noticed that I had left the driver's side window down.

We had travelled to Byron to experience the pristine waters crashing onto the sand, but I didn't think that they would end up in our car.

The seat was so wet that when you pressed it, a wave formed, and instead of heading out to sea, it headed towards the back headrest.

The staff members at reception were great. They saw me looking like a drowned rat as I entered, and once they heard that my wife had left the window down, they loaded me up with beach towels to soak up our own Lake Byron. Even though I sat on all ten beach towels, the water still seeped through, making the trip to Nimbin quite uncomfortable and somewhat damp to say the least.

Our second mistake was that we decided to let Siri take us on the scenic route. The trip normally takes just over an hour via Bangalow Road, but Siri decided our best route and the most direct route was inland. An unmade bitumen road would have spoilt us, as this inland route was filled with potholes and stretches where only loose stones provided a sturdy base for our hire car. The rain continued, as did our dodging of the potholes. Well, almost all anyway. The one-hour travel time clicked over to two hours as we arrived at Nimbin, shell-shocked and my backside soaked through. Siri was obviously having a bad day and wanted to take it out on someone. She certainly took it out on us.

The only enjoyable part of the inland route was that as we drove past numerous farms and houses, people were out the front waving. This happened at least twenty times. We are not really sure why. Perhaps they might've thought we were part of a car rally, or perhaps not many people listen to Siri now and the house owners were just happy to see anyone.

Nimbin seemed quiet. Not a hippy in sight. Perhaps hippies aren't as stupid as us to go out into the rain.

As we got out of the car with our rain jackets becoming our newest fashion headwear, my daughter mentioned a hissing sound coming from the passenger side of the car. As I walked around to investigate, the tyre went down before my very eyes.

Just as I let out a few expletives, a nice gentleman, perhaps snickering inside, advised that the service station around the corner would change the tyre for me. On three tyres and one wheel rim, we did a U-turn and headed for the garage.

Alas, our information was wrong. The service station attendant advised that they didn't change tyres, and that we would have to call the NRMA (National Roads and Motorists' Association).

As it was still raining, even though so slightly now, my wife rang the NRMA from her mobile, while I called the hire company from my phone. I was the first to be connected, but the advice that I was provided was not so well received. It was suggested that we drive to their depot in Lismore, a thirty-minute drive at best—and on three tyres, probably a lot more—let alone the damage it would incur.

Kerri waited on the phone for what was now forty minutes until I thought, "Hang on. I think I could change it. I haven't changed a tyre for over forty years, but surely it's like riding a bike. You never forget." You will be happy to know that it only took me twenty minutes, and offered the opportunity to teach Tara the finer points of changing a tyre, such as placing the new tyre under the car in case the jack collapsed. Kerri finally hung up after sixty minutes of listening to ridiculous and incredulous music on hold.

As not a lot was happening in Nimbin, we headed to Lismore for lunch, keeping a lookout for tyre retailers so that we could purchase a replacement. Unfortunately, they all closed at midday, so we had a job for Monday to look forward to. We returned to our resort by about 3 pm. My backside was beginning to dry out, but a nice shower and a change of clothes made me feel human again. Our first day in Byron was an eventful one. Expect the unexpected.

That evening, we headed into town for dinner, amazed at the choices Byron had to offer. We entered one of the many arcades, and Tara liked the look of the first restaurant we walked past. It was very well presented with indoor plants and many species of vegetation placed strategically between the tables. Prepared to accept Tara's recommendation—of course, you don't question a twenty-four-year old—we took a seat and were immediately greeted by, as we found out later, the owner.

I ordered a Coca-Cola but was quickly advised that they didn't have Coke. I apologized, saying that I couldn't drink organic cola, assuming that would be her next suggestion.

TYPICAL SHOP IN BYRON BAY

Well, I was wrong. They didn't have that either. She suggested her take on ginger beer, and because I'm a keen drinker of the non-alcoholic Bundaberg ginger beer, I accepted.

The menu was strange. I am a steak and chips man, hold the salad, but the choices were far from that. In fact, the only dish I recognized was some potato curry. Obviously not a time to be picky, so I sipped my ginger beer. I don't know what stopped me from spitting it out as I began to dry retch. What in God's name was this?

Just as I was about to comment, the owner appeared and asked for our orders. I politely remarked that the menu was very unique, and she advised that they were a 'PLANT BASED' restaurant. What a way to finish our first day in Byron Bay!

Expect the unexpected.

Life turned to normal the following day. Byron at its best.

A slight humidity filled the air, but the sunshine was electric.

We headed to the beach for the first time, only to find a busker playing on the lawn on a hill looking down to the ocean.

A group had started to gather and grew in numbers as

each song was delivered with his incredible talent.

The show lasted for around thirty minutes, and when he took a break, and I dropped a $10 note into his makeshift bank.

He probably would have more if it wasn't a cashless society.

Byron is unpredictable, and that adds to its uniqueness.

Now down to the beach. The water had a coldness to it that sent shivers through your body. However, once you got used to it, it was quite serene.

We spent the afternoon there, admiring the view and commenting that the ocean was in its ideal place, instead of inside my car.

Cape Byron Lighthouse is a must-see. So too is the trail up to it, and the scenery surrounding it.

Built at the turn of the nineteenth century, Cape Byron Lighthouse is situated on the

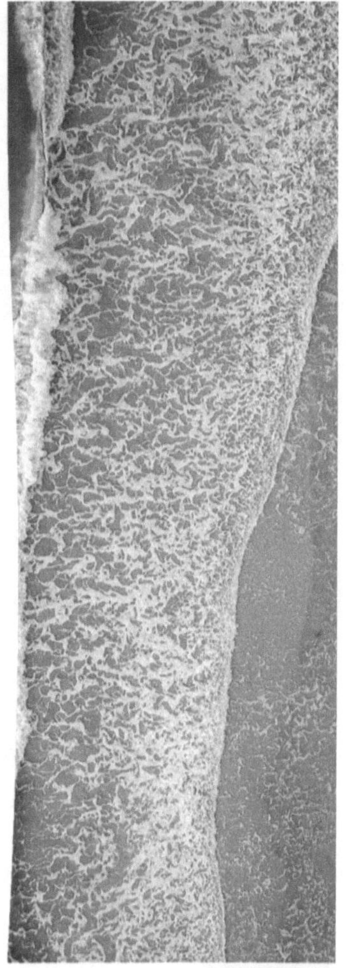

BYRON BAY

most easterly point of the Australian mainland. Operated by resident keepers until the 1980s, it's now an automated light and is visible from the Byron Bay township.

We commenced our journey to the lighthouse with brisk endeavours and at a good pace. You'll need a good two hours to properly experience the Cape Byron walking track; however, though every inch provided inspiration to go further, I was beginning to slow down.

The brochure says, "Don't be surprised if you reach the

end and feel like doing it all again." Don't believe everything you read. That was not going to happen.

The 3.7 km loop has you trekking through rainforest and across clifftops with stunning views of the ocean and hinterland.

BYRON BAY LIGHTHOUSE

The track provides shade from the Bangalow palms, as well as open spaces leaving you exposed to the hot sun's rays at times. My first thought when I reached the top and saw the car park was that I wished I had driven.

We looked out to the water, hoping to see dolphins but to no avail. I think it has to be in the right season.

If you'd prefer an easier walk, the track can be accessed at numerous points and walked in shorter sections. I wish I had known that before walking the whole track.

The pool at Elements of Byron was a big hit with my twenty-four-year-old daughter and my wife, Kerri.

Luckily, we were blessed with the weather, and it gave me some time to relax in our villa, on my own. Sometimes I like my own company. In fact, I do love it perhaps more than I should.

Whilst Byron has everything you would wish for in a relaxing holiday, you do have good access to other locations within reach, as long as you have a car.

Coolangatta and Tweed Heads will take you only forty-five minutes. Byron to Coffs Harbour, just over two hours, and let us not forget the Byron Hinterland, which is full of rolling hills, rainforests, and quaint little towns.

My five must sees and dos in Byron Bay

1. The Byron Bay Lighthouse

2. Kayak tour with dolphins and turtles

3. Nimbin (but not on a rainy day)

4. Minyon Waterfall

5. Surf lesson (make sure you don't forget to take your swimming costume)

MANILA, PHILIPINES

My advice: expect the unexpected.

TAAL VOLCANO

The Philippines is famous for the island of Boracay, its pristine waters, and its resorts and beaches. This small island is a tourist's heaven with the majority of beaches surrounded by palm trees, bars, and restaurants.

On the east coast, strong winds make Bulabog Beach a hub for water sports. Offshore, coral reefs and shipwrecks are home to diverse marine life.

Taal Volcano is the smallest active volcano in the world and is located in the freshwater Taal Lake, about fifty kilometres south of Manila. The volcano continues to emit hot fumes and ashes to this day. '*Get your guide,*' who supplied this photo, conducts day trips, and more, to this exotic location.

So, now that I have covered some extraordinary tourist destinations, let me talk about the specifics of my trip to Manila.

I am not sure why I came to the decision to visit Manila. I wanted to get away, clear my head, and start a health regime, as I had no motivation to do it at home. The weather appealed to me, as did the affordable price, as I wanted to stay for four weeks so that I could achieve my goals. It was 2021, and Melbourne had received the unwanted tag of the most locked down city in the world.

For no reason that I am aware of, I chose Chinatown, maybe because it was the heart of Manila, perhaps because it was central, although I must stipulate, this was not going to be a holiday. I had my goals and my motivation was to achieve them. Most tourists stay at Makati, home to beautiful hotels, high-rise residential buildings, nightclubs, shopping, and the financial hub of the Philippines.

But I chose Chinatown. Expect the unexpected.

CHINATOWN

I arrived in Manila around four in the afternoon and was surprised to experience the United States Marines, carrying out the border checks, immigration, etc. As is normal, as soon as you leave the feeling of apprehension of immigration, even though you are not carrying anything illegal, the doors open and you are thrust into the manic hysteria of taxis wanting your business, dignitaries waiting to be picked up in limousines, and families waiting for loved ones. You take a deep breath and look for your name on a card for your prebooked transport to the hotel. I was approached by the scout for taxis but I explained that I had a prebooked car waiting for me. After thirty minutes of waiting, I called Viator, who had taken my booking and money, only to find that no booking existed even though I had a reservation number and receipt. I tracked down the taxi scout with my tail between my legs, and after abusing Viator, headed to Chinatown via taxi.

The thirty-five-minute trip took one hour and thirty minutes, due to the traffic; I made a mental note of this for my return to the airport in four weeks.

As we drove into Chinatown, it was like every other Chinatown I had visited before. Food stalls and street food kiosks set up with little stoves burning, putting pressure on one single candle to cook and keep the food simmering all day.

If only candles could talk. We arrived at the hotel, my home for the next four weeks.

There were many restaurants nearby, and the 7-Eleven next door was a godsend, as I needed to stock the minibar with water in the thirty-two degree humid heat.

The hotel was located across the road from Binondo Church, formally known as the Minor Basilica and National Shrine of Saint Lorenzo Ruiz. The church was founded by Dominican priests in 1596.

Although destroyed in 1762 by British bombardment, a new granite church was completed on the same site in 1852, which was also damaged during the second world war. However, it is worth a visit. The internal fixtures are beautiful, and choir voices could be heard from my hotel room on a regular basis.

My routine was set. Up at 6 am, coffee in the room, then off to Rizal Park. The heat had an impact on you immediately. Even at 6 am, it was thirty degrees, with a really humid bite to it. Rizal Park was beautiful—but it was somewhat strange to find a park of this size and beauty in the middle of a concrete jungle.

Whilst Rizal Park was the name of the whole park precinct, Luneta Park was a small area branching off to the south. This is where I discovered my quiet running and walking track that I diligently visited every day for four weeks.

PHOTO OUT OF APARTMENT WINDOW ONTO BINONDO CHURCH

SECURITY AND MYSELF AT HOTEL RAMADA BINONDO

The daily walk gave me a great appreciation of life in Manila. It was like stepping through different movie sets. Leaving the business district of Binondo, you'd pass the little alleyways with vendors selling fresh fruit and cold drinks, some made of concoctions you'd never heard of before—and truth be known, didn't want to hear of again.

The closest park to the hotel was 3.5 km away, 5 km if you get lost, which was a regular occurrence every day for one week. It was only after one week that I started to recognize critical landmarks.

RIZAL PARK

COVID was still a big issue in the Philippines. Everyone wore masks inside and out; in fact, there was a fine if you didn't. I had taken a reusable mask with me, but clearly, that was not going to be enough to last the four weeks.

I headed to the local market, about 500 metres from Chinatown. Well, what an array of masks and colours. Fashion statements, being sold in packs of ten, twenty, or fifty. To reflect my mood, I chose black. Enter problem number one. It was difficult to determine which was the inside, which was the outside, and which way was up or down. After two days of trying to work it out, I decided to buy a white marker pen, so that I could mark each one to alleviate my problem.

The region of Binondo was broken into streets that sold the same products, where each competitor had their shops next door to each other. In other words, one street was for stationery, and as school was about to recommence, these streets were packed to the rafters.

One street would sell electronics only, another T-shirts and hoodies, another kitchenware, etc. What I found is that a very minimal number of these vendors spoke English.

Here was I standing in a queue of shoppers, in one of the stationery streets, trying to explain that I needed a pen or bottle that contained white paint to make corrections to mistakes with something that we called Tipp-Ex or Wite-Out. It was not easy, but Marcel Marceau would have been very impressed. Finally, my message got through, and the next 400 people in the queue were able to move forward.

The only person I met in the shops who spoke good English was in a T-shirt and hoodie shop. My eye caught a nice, and cheap, maroon hoodie. I asked to try it on and requested my normal size, a large. Well, I couldn't even get it over my head. She brought me an XL, which wasn't that much better. I asked if she had anything bigger, and she replied that she didn't because I was too fat. I never looked for hoodies again.

While talking about shopping, there are numerous food and clothing markets within a one-kilometre radius of Chinatown. Each was a Coronavirus mega spreader, but no one seemed to care, as long as they were wearing their masks. At one stage, I felt I had another layer of skin because I was so close to the other shoppers looking for bargains. Think now of all of this intimacy in thirty-degree humid heat.

Each market seemed to join at various points, but my favourite was the Tutuban night market. I am not sure if it was because of the atmosphere that a night market delivers, or if it was the bargains and variety that was on offer. I bought runners for all the family, and some even lasted for a month.

I purposely didn't take my phone to Manila with me, as I was concerned about losing it, or at worse, having to pay the exorbitant roaming fees. As an organized person, I purchased a 4G Mobile for about $50 from electrical retailer, Harvey Norman. This would do the trick, until I got to Manila and tried to buy a SIM card, again with all vendors in the one street. None sold the SIM cards, and I tried every shop. They were all 5G, very much ahead of where we were in Australia. At least I got $30 for it when I returned to Australia. But of course, with no phone, it meant no navigation. With no navigation, I got lost on a very regular basis.

TUTUBAN NIGHT MARKET

Eating, especially in Chinatown, provides numerous choices, especially if you like Chinese food.

It wasn't long until I had locked in my regulars. For dumplings, more so at lunchtime or early evening, Dong Bei was my choice. Pork and kuchay were all P200 (pesos) or $5 AUD for servings of generally five. I also took a liking for xia long bao. Xia is a type of small Chinese steamed bun traditionally prepared in a xiaolong, a small bamboo steaming basket.

The President Grand Palace was my 'go to' restaurant to spoil myself. Whilst I think the locals were given priority over Westerners when service came to mind, the food was excellent.

THE PRESIDENT GRAND PALACE RESTAURANT

My favourite dish was rice with salt and pepper calamari.

Around the corner at Eng Bee, downstairs was like a Chinese deli, with upstairs being a restaurant. As I found out, they didn't sell Coke Zero, but they let me go next door to the 7-Eleven to buy some. They had some spectacular duck dishes, and their staff, while quite young, were very accommodating and there to please. They had a big Buddha in the foyer of the delicatessen and would laugh when I came up the stairs. They said that I reminded them of the big Buddha but in a nice way. It was only when the staff wanted to rub my belly, as it was good luck, that I became embarrassed.

Finally, I must mention Chuan Kee. It is situated on Ongpin Road and opens at about 11 am. By 11:30 am, the queues wind around the streets, sometimes 50 metres long.

They made an incredible tasting mango smoothie, which I religiously consumed after my walk or often for lunch, although the crowds were there for their quick and unique Chinese street food.

I had been in Manila for about two weeks when I discovered a lovely local, selling fresh pineapple. She would cut it up for me and place it in a cellophane bag, so each day, I would buy four (they were so cheap), and give the other three to the security guards and staff at the hotel. I have never, and will probably never again, taste pineapple as fresh as this was. It gave me motivation to finish my walk, knowing what was waiting for me at the end.

Some would think that I had a foot fetish. I had purchased a pair of Nike sneakers—well, they had a Nike badge on them, at Tutuban market. As I was walking around twelve kilometres each day, my feet were starting to hurt when I would get back to the hotel each evening. If you think buying Tipp-Ex was hard enough, try describing an orthotic insole to someone who doesn't speak English. My description without words was exceptional, and finally, I was given directions to an orthotic shop in the complex called 'Lucky Chinatown' which comprised about fifty shops in a setting similar to a Westfield. You can imagine me on one foot, pointing to my shoes, placing my hand at right angles to the ground, and slipping my fingers into my shoe.

The next day, it was raining, and out I went, wearing my leather shoes to protect me from having wet feet. All was going well until I slipped because the tread on my shoes had worn, and nearly ended up on my backside and right in the middle of a large puddle.

The hotel staff were great when I told them. Immediately, they summoned a motorbike and a rider and told him to take me somewhere to get a new sole for my leather shoes. He drove for what seemed like an hour until he stopped at the curb of a little side street. Lying adjacent to the curb was an old man in his eighties, who was fast asleep on the footpath. The rider woke him up and spoke to him in Filipino; he rose to his feet, grabbed my shoes, and sat on a little four-legged stool, while he started to cut rubber by hand. It took him thirty minutes with precision cutting and gluing in a posture that would have had me trying to stand up for days. He wanted to charge me P180, the equivalent of $5, but I gave him more so that he could afford to buy his own shoes.

OLD STYLE COBBLER

As an animal lover, I was curious to see many pets going into a shop diagonally opposite my hotel. When I queried this with one of the porters, he advised that it might be a vet. This, of course, seemed a little out of place because of the amount of stray dogs and cats roaming the streets. I would cringe whenever I saw one trying to cross the road, with the maniac taxis and drivers feeling it was more important to dodge the potholes in the road rather than these innocent animals.

Expect the unexpected.

On one of my many walks to the park, I walked over one of the bridges that provided a passage over the murky and disgusting rivers heading out to Manila Bay. There lying on the footpath was a dead cat; it appeared that it had been hit by a car, and someone had thoughtfully placed it into a heavenly resting position.

For the next three days, I walked on the other side of the road, as mentally I couldn't handle walking past it every day. I even contemplated paying a council-employed worker to remove it, even after the staff at the hotel said councils don't do that type of thing.

Anyway, one week out from returning home, I crossed back to the normal route on my way to the park. I could see some ball in the gutter and was curious to identify it. As I got closer, I could see it was a kitten about the size of an iPhone. I assumed it was dead, and my heart sank when I thought I would be confronted with another situation like before. I went up to it and started whistling. Its ear twitched. I was conscious of not picking it up in my hands due to our strict biosecurity and quarantine laws. I luckily had a face washer from the hotel, and proceeded to pick up the kitten, wrapping it in the face washer. It was thirty-five degrees, maybe forty- five degrees in the gutter, so I saw some vendors manning their carts around the corner and quickly bought a bottle of cold water. The kitten started to drink, slowly at first, then with vigor after a few minutes. Holding the kitten out from my chest, I walked back to around the ten vendors asking if they wanted a kitten. Unsurprisingly, they said no. Just then, and before panic set in, I remembered the vet that was across the road from the hotel.

The kitten was starting to make some squeaking sounds as I took off with my arms outstretched on a two kilometre run to hopefully save my newfound friend. As I got to the vet, I stopped, and disappointment hit me when I saw it wasn't a vet, but a mortgage broker. I immediately thought that my only chance was to take the kitten to my hotel and get them to look after it in the hotel basement. Suddenly, I looked up and a man was gesturing me towards him. The vet was five doors down.

He opened the door for me, and like Moses parting the Red Sea, all the patients in front of me with an abundance of a variety of animals allowed me to reach the counter.

I explained the situation and advised that the kitten was in urgent need of help, and I was more than happy to pay for it. Immediately, it was taken away to be hydrated. They advised that the kitten would be ready to be picked up the following day, but I explained that I was heading back to Australia. I asked how much it would cost to find a good home. When told it would cost P9,000, I didn't hesitate. For $250 AUD, it was well worth it. I returned to the vet the next day, only to be shown the kitten in its cage climbing and meowing around, and full of so much energy that I had a tear in my eye.

I never went back again, as I could do no more. Expect the unexpected.

My five must sees and dos in Manila

1. Binondo Chinatown

2. Tutuban Night Market

3. Pagsanjan Falls

4. Taal Volcano

5. Makati Region

BARCELONA, SPAIN

My advice: expect the unexpected.

Barcelona is Spain's exciting city filled with art and architecture. It's the birthplace of Picasso and Salvador Dalí and home to the 'yet to be finished' La Sagrada Familia, which commenced construction in 1882.

It is amazing the reaction you get when you tell someone that you are off to Barcelona. It is a must for your bucket list as there is no other city like it in the world. Yet, as mentioned earlier, even the seasoned traveller can experience those moments that they were not expecting and have no control over.

ANTIQUE LOOKING STAIRWAY AT OUR APARTMENT

Forty-five hours had passed since we left home and arrived at our apartment in Gran Via, Barcelona, at 1 am. We were tired, excited, anxious, and let me say again, TIRED and exhausted. Our instructions were clear. Put the code 1985 into the key box, where you will find two keys. Take only the one with the number three on it. That is for your apartment. The other one is for another guest.

We were well prepared. My wife's role was to watch the cases while we stood in the street, as it was now 1:15 am and Barcelona does have a bad reputation for crime, founded or unfounded. My daughter's role was to hold her mobile with the torch turned on, and my responsibility was the key box, which is not as easy as you think when you have fat fingers.

Everything was falling into place, like clockwork, you might say, as it was now 1:30 am. The roads were quiet and two homeless people seemed to be settled in for the night.

To our amazement, there was only one key in the key box. Had the other guests arrived earlier? We entered the old-fashioned lift that was barely large enough to accommodate us and the suitcases. We closed the wrought-iron gate on the lift first, followed by the beautiful heavy-grained walnut door.

Signs are everywhere.

"If you don't close properly, the lift will not operate."

FRONT FAÇADE OF APARTMENT BLOCK

We reached our floor and attempted to open our apartment three door. No. The key doesn't work. Perhaps the other guests had taken our key by mistake. We looked at our watches. It was now 2 am. Exhausted and now irritable, we knocked on the door to apartment three to no avail. It was

VIEW FROM OUR BALCONY

then that I noticed a number one on the back of the key. It fitted the door to apartment one, so we decided that we would sleep there overnight, but not unpack, and contact the off-site manager in the morning. At 12 midday, she finally responded to our texts. Sorry, Allan. I thought apartment one would suit you better, so I put you in there. Unfortunately, she forgot to tell us. Expect the unexpected. Welcome to Spain.

If Barcelona and Madrid are on your bucket list, bring them to the top of the pile. Both cities are amazing, although Madrid was our least favourite.

A brief reconnaissance the next morning to familiarise ourselves with the surroundings proved beneficial and showed the importance of a centrally situated hotel. In our case, it was a two-bedroom, beautifully fitted-out apartment, as we were accompanied by our twenty-three-year-old daughter. Anyway, after a hearty breakfast and coffee (we asked for a croissant with JAM and received a croissant with HAM), we set off on our discovery tour of Barcelona. My daughter had broken the map of the city into coloured quadrants and after reading

Lonely Planet and getting feedback from previous tourists, we allocated each quadrant to a particular day. Having children to do this is essential, as I definitely would not have had the patience.

We are seasoned travellers, but most of the feedback we received on Barcelona was focused on safety, so much so that we became paranoid and bought everything from passport holders that hang around your neck to money purses that sit around your waist under your clothes, as well as bum bags and knapsacks that sit around your chest rather than on your back. Yes, be diligent with safety. Don't put your phone on the table or your bag on the chair, and don't tempt fate with the numerous pickpockets by carrying lots of cash. But Barcelona is no different from anywhere else in the world; albeit, they have the best pickpockets in the world, especially as the tourists were returning after COVID. Don't let it consume your holiday or ruin it. We didn't have any trouble, apart from having to carry all these Korjo safety products on us and it being extremely uncomfortable.

First stop was the Picasso Museum. I am not a lover of art, especially when Picasso paints three heads on a body and square faces on shoulders with no necks. What I didn't realize was that at fifteen he was a master, and his talent was unbelievable. It was only when he got older that his creativity went haywire, in my opinion. It is worth the visit and paying extra to get an audio guide.

I took this photo on our phone. Picasso painted it at fifteen years of age. When you stand back from the painting, you can make out the text in the book that she is holding. However, as you get closer, the words disappear into lines.

If the name Gaudí doesn't mean anything to you, it certainly will by the time you leave Barcelona.

We started the day with breakfast at a café, which gave us good choices of Western food. Our palates don't and can't take the Spanish options such as tortilla de patatas (potato

THE FIRST COMMUNION

and onion omelettes). I tend to be a plain egg and toast man, but if you like a mix of sweet and savoury foods, Spain is the place for you.

We might've questioned smoking restrictions around some cities in the world, especially around food venues when they were first introduced, but Spain, along with many parts of Europe, is the extreme that you will need to adjust to. Clear air doesn't appear to be an option.

If you decide to sit outside, which is always my favourite option, you will need to compete with the smokers. I gave up smoking forty years ago but felt like I was back to smoking a packet a day because at €5 a packet ($8 AUD), passive smoke filled the air while you were having breakfast, lunch, or dinner.

I discovered a 6 am coffee spot. Great coffee, as close as I have found to a weak latte, filled with construction workers with early starts, and midnight revellers still finding energy and voice from the night before. I sat there quietly sipping my coffee and enjoying listening to the Spanish-speaking locals and had no idea what they were saying. It was entertaining though, and such an experience. This was better than lying in bed.

The owner of the café started to know how I took my coffee. She didn't understand a weak latte, but she did understand a latte not strong. We got there in the end.

Back to the apartment to wake

COFFEE SHOP AT 6 AM

up the girls, have a shower, and attack the first quadrant, which was filled with Gaudí influences and architecture ahead of its time. NO HOT WATER. Can you believe it? I texted the manager again and off we went to our list of must-dos in Barcelona. A cold shower does get the heart started.

We commenced in the city, where we walked past Casa Milà aka La Pedrera, Casa Amatller, which was previously an old chocolate factory, and Mercat de la Boqueria, a local market with food stalls and everything you could wish for. As I walked past the confectionery stall, the sweet smell hit me, and I could already taste my favourites without putting them into my mouth. A nice cool drink with numerous choices was just the tonic in the oppressive heat. Beads of sweat were a constant fashion accessory that followed you wherever you went. We received a call from the manager of the apartment. The hot water service had blown up, and it would take two days to replace. However, all was not lost. We had been given permission to shower in apartment twenty-one. What? Here we were walking down the corridor from our apartment to apartment twenty-one in our towels because we didn't take dressing gowns with us. After all, the space in our suitcases can be used to buy more shoes, as I was reminded by the females.

A guided tour of Palau de la Música Catalana ensured we saw and received information on pieces of history that we may otherwise have missed. The guide was sensational. She was from Germany, and the mixture of accents from Germany and Spain were intriguing and unique; you hung on every word as a result.

She walked us around town. Through the Gothic Quarter where the streets were so narrow, you could almost touch the wall from one side of the laneway to the other side with your arms outstretched. The Jewish Quarter was filled with history and little shops inconspicuously positioned with staff waiting

BARCELONA STREET   JEWISH QUARTER

for the next customer.

Lunch on Las Ramblas (one of the main tourist thoroughfares in Barcelona) consisted of more tapas platters, but the quality so far had been exceptional.

Must-sees in this area were La Catedral and Plaça de Sant Just, yet another iconic square, which also accommodates this building in the photo adjacent, full of character and history.

Just imagine standing in front of this iconic building and walking down the same street where Eulàlia, patron saint of Barcelona, was tortured during the period of persecution of Christians.

Plaça del Rei and Basílica de Santa Maria del Mar are further destinations that cannot be left off

PLACA DE SANT JUST

your list. We spent the day visiting La Catedral (this is not a spelling error) and Plaça de Sant Jaume.

Somehow, two thousand years old just seems like a number, until the reality of the age really sinks in.

Whenever you mention to anyone that you are going to Barcelona, the normal response is "When is La Sagrada going to be finished?" It isn't fair. It's only been 140 years since it first started, with Gaudí being the chief architect. Although, I did see a construction worker who looked like he was there from the start. After all, the Cologne Cathedral took 632 years to build and the Melbourne Airport Link will probably take longer.

La Sagrada Familia is a church designed by architect Gaudí (1852–1926), and commenced on 19 March 1882, although initially under the guise of architect Francisco de Paula del Villar. In 1883, when Villar resigned, Gaudí took over as chief architect, devoting the remainder of his life to the project, and he is buried in the church's crypt. At the time of his death in 1926, less than a quarter of the project was complete. Gaudí died a pauper when hit by a tram.

We organised a tour and prebooked before we left, as the crowds can be horrendous. It is a sight to be seen, which is ironic because you can pretty well see it from every locale in Barcelona.

LA SAGRADA FAMILIA

This is not just another church. The outside is spectacular, but as the following pictures show, the internals leave nothing to the imagination.

We left this extraordinary structure and headed to another Gaudí creation. Words cannot describe this either, but pictures will create a thousand words. This is Casa Battló.

Casa Batlló was considered one of Gaudí's greatest masterpieces. The local name for Casa Batlló is Casa dels ossos or House of Bones. The only bones I saw were the ones I felt after walking twelve kilometres on our third day. It was built

CASA BATLLÓ

in the most expensive real estate area of Barcelona.

Again, a tour group is a good idea because it does get you into some areas that the public is normally not allowed.

We are attacking the fourth quadrant today, highlighted in orange on our map. More walking. After checking my app showing distances travelled, I saw that we were averaging around twelve kilometres per day. My legs were weary, and I could feel every sore and strained muscle on each hill, which there were many of.

We visited The University of Barcelona, which was draped in history, magnificent architecture, and lots of grandeur stairs; I felt every step as we climbed them.

Off to Montjuïc Castle and yes, more stairs. We took the train, which was very easy to navigate, although a lovely old man offered us guidance, even though he spoke no English. On arrival, we walked past the Magic Fountain, Museum Nacional d'Art de Catalunya, and looked back in amazement at the magnificent view of Barcelona. Castell de Montjuïc is a huge fortress at the top of the mountain. There was a small event situated on one of the lawns as we approached, and within

TOP: BARCELONA
UNIVERSITY FACADE

RIGHT: BARCELONA
UNIVERSITY

five minutes, we were sitting on the grass munching on a ham baguette. A ham baguette in Barcelona. Who would've believed that?

From this elevation and with more stairs, I could see my dream: Barcelona Football Stadium! I had seen an advertisement for an upcoming game of soccer and was trying to think of an excuse that I could use to entice my wife into letting me go and watch. I stood there mesmerized, looking down on this magnificent stadium, and dreaming of putting on the blue and garnet football shirt. It was only after we got back to our apartment and looked back on our adventures that I realized I was actually looking at the Arenas de Barcelona, a local shopping centre that used to be used for bullfighting. Embarrassed and somewhat disappointed, I found that the stadium was in fact two kilometres away.

Dinner, sitting outside, comprised of BBQ beef tacos followed by a dessert of profiteroles and vanilla millefeuille, which helped me forget my Barca FC (Football Club) experience.

There is so much to see in this tourist mecca. I have only covered a few places. We loved Casa Lleó Morera, Casa Sagnier, and Casa Serra.

This, of course, adds to the benefit of having a daughter who is prepared to create a map broken into quadrants. You get to see everything, including the beach at El Poblenou. Only a few stops from Barcelona Metro, this beach has pristine waters and cafes spread along the sand, adjacent to the footpaths, giving you access from the road and the beach. Be mindful that there is a nude beach when on a direct route to the beach from the station. I was quite happy to settle there for the day, but my wife dragged me away using some excuse about whiter sand a few hundred metres down the beach and being closer to the cafes.

Expect the unexpected.

I could write a whole story filled with information about the uniqueness of the food available to you in Spain. Whilst you see signs at every second café for tapas, there is plenty of variation available under the umbrella title that encompasses that of tapas. Western breakfasts were a little more challenging, but subsequently, the benefit of that was that we got to know one of the waiters very well at a café we frequented on several occasions.

Through broken English, he had a sensational sense of humour. Back to dinner. Some of the meals we experienced were delicacies such as grilled octopus with potatoes, crab cannelloni, lobster, fried eggplant, churros with chocolate souffle,

TOP: ENTRANCE TO CASTELL DE MONTJUIC

LEFT: THE MAGNIFICENT BARCELONA FOOTBALL STADIUM THAT TURNS OUT NOT TO BE THE MAGNIFICENT BARCELONA FOOTBALL STADIUM.

pulled pork tacos, calamari, and even "prosciutto pizza." One important thing to note is that Spaniards tend to eat dinner later, such as around anywhere between 8 pm and 10 pm, with the latter quite the norm. As a result, lunch is eaten around 2 pm to 3 pm, with little emphasis on breakfast. Croissants and baguettes appear to be the breakfasts on most menus.

The weather was exceptional. We had missed the forty-degree days in August/September and were experiencing thirty degrees, which we were comfortable with, although it could

LOCAL RESTAURANT BARCELONA

be a little humid, especially at night. As a result of the good weather, the majority of cafes and restaurants had an abundance of outdoor seating, whether it be in the middle of the hustle and bustle of Las Ramblas, enjoying the serenity of the quieter south Las Ramblas, or the many cute and eclectic eating places hidden in some of the laneways and side streets.

We also heard before we arrived in Spain that shops close for fiesta between 2 pm and 4 pm. Our guide told us that was the case in the olden days, when people usually lived above their shops and were the only ones working, so they needed to take a break. Now they can't afford to.

Casa Comalat is a Gaudi influenced heritage building, as is Palau Guell, the interior of which is extraordinary. Baró de Quadras, a small modernista palace, and Palau Ramon Montaner, built in 1893, are also must-sees.

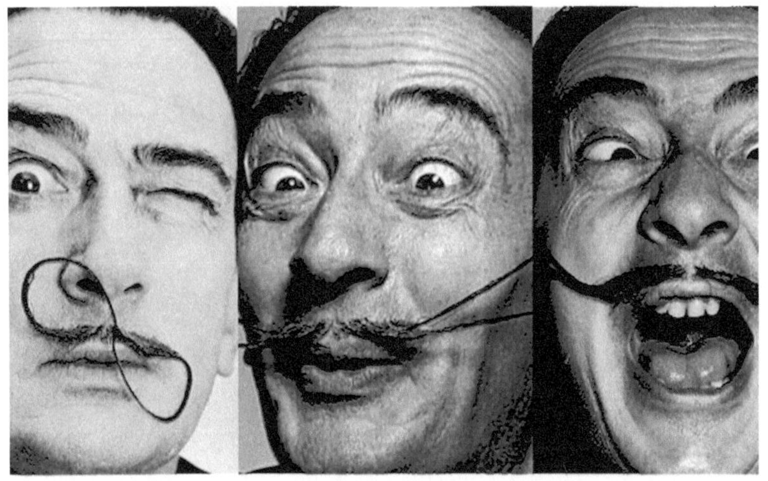

Salvador Dalí

The Salvador Dalí Museum in Figueres is probably more of a wish than a "must do." However, when we researched all our options, we were desperate to fit it into our itinerary, and I would highly recommend it. We hired a driver and vehicle, which offered either 120 kilometres or six hours. As Figueres was at least one hour from Barcelona, I deduced that with two hours of travelling time, two at the museum, and perhaps a bite of lunch, the second option was the best.

Unfortunately, I misread the terms and conditions. What it actually meant was that the six hours could be spent as long as you didn't go over 120 kilometres, so on the way, we had to renegotiate, which wasn't a pleasant experience. After all, if you push too hard, the driver is likely to leave you there.

The museum really depicted the personality of Dalí, who was strange but talented. The only regret I had was that we were only fifteen kilometres from the French border. If I had known that, I would have loved to pop over the border for lunch.

By mistake, we didn't pre-organize a tour. In hindsight, I

do feel we would've got a lot more out of the visit. The system in place was very disjointed, in that you moved within the museum by rooms, numerically labelled. I found that we were more focused on the next room number, rather than the works themselves. However, I did notice my wife studying a photo of Dalí in the nude. She spent at least five minutes staring at it. Perhaps that was because we have been married for forty years.

The artwork on the next page was created using different elements that appeared randomly placed when viewed from the side. It was only when you moved ninety degrees around the room that the perspective changed to form the face. Quite ingenious, really. We returned to Barcelona and the driver was very quiet and steely.

THE REAL BARCELONA FOOTBALL STADIUM

MARILYN MONROE ROOM

My five must sees and dos in Barcelona

1. Casa Battló

2. La Sagrada Familia

3. Picasso Museum

4. Mercat de la Boqueria

5. Gothic Quarter

MADRID, SPAIN

My advice: expect the unexpected.

The bullet train to Madrid was a great option. It only took two hours and thirty minutes and cost between €50 and €150 ($80 AUD to $245 AUD), depending on the time you were departing and the class of travel. First class was called preferente, and the second class was referred to as turista. At the entrance of each carriage, there was an unsecured luggage area, which meant that you were separated from your luggage. Whilst most would panic under these circumstances, it seemed to work, as our luggage was still there when we went back to collect it.

The train trip was comfy, and there were also drink and snack options on board, albeit in a separate carriage.

As we headed for the taxi ranks, there had to be over 500 taxis waiting in two parallel lines, and probably just as many passengers hoping for a smooth transition.

As we lined up in an orderly fashion, even though there was no official

TARA OUTSIDE THE BEAR AND THE STRAWBERRY TREE STATUE IN PUERTA DEL SOL

directing traffic, approximately ten taxis drove up to the start of the line to collect the next passenger.

As the taxis banked up, instead of the next lot of passengers waiting for the next taxi to drive up, the front of the line of passengers started heading down towards the next available taxi.

All of a sudden, we and many others were halfway (approximately fifty metres) from between the start of the queue and the next available taxi.

The next taxi then drove to the front of the queue and others in the queue moved forward, leaving us stranded and creating utter chaos.

Everyone was screaming and shouting and we had no idea what they were saying. We gathered our three bags and headed for an available taxi, but he refused to take us, because 'we had too much luggage.'

About 200 metres back in the waiting area, we could see an eight-seater taxi, so we headed towards that, but the driver was constantly shaking his head, which was universally known as NO, and refused to take us. He kept pointing for us to go to the front of the line, which we had visited fifteen minutes earlier.

My patience had run out. I suggested to my wife that she stand in front of that taxi, blocking his chance to move and putting her at risk, while I opened the boot and lifted our luggage without him having any choice. OK, so we paid for it. He screeched around corners, exceeded the speed limit tenfold, and got us to our hotel in five minutes, which I have come to learn normally takes fifteen minutes. Expect the unexpected. Welcome to Madrid.

We reached our room in a beautiful 4.5 star hotel, just around the corner from Plaza de la Puerta del Sol, a very central location.

It was about thirty degrees outside, and the same inside, so I switched the air conditioner from heat to cool, switched it on, and we left the room to explore and have some dinner. Tapas again, but tapas in Madrid is not like anywhere else in the world, apart from Barcelona. Anyway, the dulce de leche, a sort of caramelized milk concoction for dessert, took away the taste we had experienced and been accustomed to for the last week. I must admit that I was becoming a bit 'tapassed out.'

FAÇADE HOTEL CATALONIA
PUERTA DEL SOL

We returned to the hotel some two hours later, only to find that the room hadn't cooled down. I suggested to my wife that we should complain to reception, but she commented that we wouldn't notice it if we slept with a sheet only. When we awoke in a sweat, I headed to reception. A maintenance man arrived thirty minutes later and approached the control panel. He switched from cool to heat and started to leave our room. Bewildered, I asked what I had done wrong. In broken English, he apologised and explained that three years ago, the hotel had undergone a renovation, and the electricians had rewired the controls back to front. If this wasn't true, you wouldn't believe it. No signs. Nothing. Anyway, our room cooled down, and the rest of our stay was pleasant.

We did experience a divide between Barcelona and Madrid. We found the Madrid people that we dealt with to be less patient and accommodating.

However, the scenery, especially the architecture, was on a

similar scale to Barcelona. Plaza de la Puerta del Sol and Plaza Mayor were enormous spaces, replicating car parks with no cars and no parking lines. They were both filled with impressive statues and surrounded by small cafes, with the majority of seating outside. This created a real and comfortable ambience, especially as the sun went down.

The following day, we headed off to Plaza de la Villa, and

PUERTA DEL SOL

on our way, encountered the Basílica Pontificia de San Miguel and a trip inside made it more special. We also discovered the ruins of the Almudena church before it was destroyed; it was a Roman Catholic cathedral that depicted Gothic architecture in the true sense of the word. We then made our way to Plaza de la Armería, where the Catedral de Nuestra Señora de la Almudena and Palacio Real are. Unfortunately, we could see the queue to the Palace from 200 metres away. This was one thing that we should have planned.

We got up early and headed 'Take Two' for the Palacio Real. Nearby, we found a lovely café that sold fresh fruit, a variety of yogurts as well as granola bowls, croissants, and a variety of fresh and unusual breads. We couldn't refuse washing our breakfast down with a coconut and pineapple smoothie, my daughter's choice, or freshly squeezed orange juices.

ROYAL PALACE OF MADRID

The Palacio Real was impressive, but there were limitations in taking photos, as it's still used for royal engagements. We saw the King's and Queen's rooms, banquet hall, and lots of artifacts on display like silverware and musical instruments, and each room was decorated very much with their own individuality. On the way back, we went into the Mercado de San Miguel and picked up some food for lunch.

Again, many choices such as a ham and cheese wrap. After a rest, we went to watch a flamenco performance. It was a really energetic mix of dancing, singing, and guitar. Quesadillas were a popular choice for dinner at a café in a small square around the corner from the theatre. This experience was very special.

Our last day began with breakfast across the road from the hotel. Our daughter had a cinnamon roll covered in lotus spread, but a croissant for me supported my plain tastes.

We had heard about the El Rastro flea market, which is certainly the largest and longest flea market I have ever seen, with well-priced new and secondhand goods, as well as limited pieces of Lladro ornaments, which were born in Spain and are extremely popular and recognisable. I recognized a piece that sells on eBay for over $1,700 AUD, but this one was just € 300, which equates to $500 AUD or $330 USD.

I was in my element. However, as the morning went on, so did the crowds. It was like being in Times Square on New Year's Eve, or St. Peter's Basilica on Easter Sunday. The market seemed to go on forever. Forty years of marriage, and I still could not convince my wife to buy a Lladro ornament. I felt like my heart had been cut out as I looked back at the Lladro, never to be seen again.

Even our next stop, the Basílica de San Francisco El Grande, with a high dome of extravagant frescoes and stained-glass windows, couldn't eliminate my disappointment.

Heading Home

An early flight had the alarm set for 1:45 am. The streets around the corner from our hotel were quite busy with people who had been clubbing. Whilst we had a magnificent holiday, and one that I would recommend highly, another forty-five-hour stint on the plane was not the challenge I had been looking forward to. Unfortunately, during our flight, there was a medical emergency on board just as I visited the toilet, meaning I couldn't return to my seat. At one point, it was looking like we would have to make an emergency landing in Turkey.

Thankfully, all ended well, and we continued on our journey.

We arrived in Melbourne only to be told that our luggage was somewhere in Singapore. As I mentioned, good planning can still not prevent things that are out of your control.

Expect the unexpected.

My five must sees and dos in Madrid

1. Plaza Mayor and Plaza de la Puerta del Sol

2. Palacio Real (The Royal Palace)

3. Mercado de San Miguel

4. Basílica de San Francisco El Grande

5. Flamenco Show (prebook)

SURFERS PARADISE, QUEENSLAND, AUSTRALIA

My advice: expect the unexpected.

SURFERS PARADISE COASTLINE

Surfers Paradise is a destination suited to and frequented by all sorts of people. It attracts the southerners who want to retire in a warmer climate with a relaxed lifestyle, the international visitors who have never experienced so much in one place, and those who regard Surfers as the go-to place, when you just need a holiday with warm weather and a destination that is within reach of most pockets and most travel distances within Australia.

Surfers, as it's known to the locals (we Australians have a habit of shortening all names), was originally called Elston. However, Jim Cavill, who purchased just twenty-five acres of land (approx. 101,000 m2) built the Surfers Paradise Hotel and lobbied hard to have the name changed to Surfers Paradise.

It is interesting to note, especially when you see so much development here, that land was extremely difficult to sell in the '30s, as access was difficult, the region being split by the Nerang River. It was only after the bridge was built that demand and developments occurred.

Surfers has changed over the years. No Charlie's on Cavill Avenue. Charlie's was the restaurant that catered to all. Breakfast, lunch, and dinner, with décor celebrating the life of Charlie Chaplin. Many of the apartment blocks, built in the boom of the 1980s, have been replaced by multiple story brand new developments, some featuring whole floors, rather than just one, two, or three bedrooms. The multiple story Grosvenor and Zenith still exist in their original forms. Many apartments owned by different vendors have been renovated, but many have not. Price varies depending on the condition of the apartment.

Surfers is a place for all ages, but especially children under the age of twelve. Movie World, Dream World, and Sea World are destinations catering to that age group, as well as the young at heart. Sanctuary Cove, Broadbeach, and Main Beach have developed with the higher socioeconomic group in mind, with a large variety of eating and shopping options available.

Investment on the Gold Coast is an interesting subject. Development seems to have been continuous since the '80s with new complexes being created on a regular basis, although well-built apartment blocks such as the Golden Gate, the Marriott, Moroccan, and Sun City have all stood the test of time.

It's now 2024 and almost all apartment blocks within a kilometre radius of Cavill Avenue have NO VACANCY signs out front. From experience though, capital growth has probably underdelivered on vendor expectations. Maybe it is because supply outweighs demand in the middle market price point. However, the amount of 'no vacancies,' outside of school holidays, would suggest that returns are consistent and there are many benefits to be had with investments as long as reliance is not on capital growth.

The state and local governments must be commended on the improvements to infrastructure from Southport down to Coolangatta.

The opening of the M1, between Brisbane and the Gold Coast, delivered easier access for Brisbanites wanting a weekend away or a day at the beach. The journey (as listed by Google) is supposed to take one hour and eighteen minutes, but the underestimated number of users have resulted in regular traffic jams, let alone accidents leading to extended travel times. I know someone who actually took one hour and nineteen minutes.

Those with weak bladders are well catered to, with every second shopping complex having public toilets and toilets positioned about 100 metres apart along the foreshore. With the introduction of a tram, access from Southport to Broadbeach brings the whole of the Gold Coast within reach.

The shops have changed also. Many fashion shops and chains have moved to Pacific Fair at Broadbeach or Australia Fair at Southport.

Now in Surfers, every second shop is a tattoo artist, convenience store, or massage business. I thought it ironic, but smart, that Phresh Ink on the Gold Coast Highway has a finger in both pies, offering a tattoo service as well as a tattoo removal service. Brilliant entrepreneurship!

PHRESH INK

I have had many memories over the years of Surfers. It was our 'go to' place as a family; sometimes we'd even drive up from Melbourne in the family's Ford Fairmont. When we had our only child, Tara, Surfers was our first holiday together, simply because of the ease of getting around.

As young adults, we would hire a 'Mini Moke,' which was cheap, but had no windows, and the makeshift roof was a tarpaulin.

I remember trying to take every opportunity to get the last bit of sun before we returned home to the cold, wet winters. One afternoon was a great example. We headed for the beach at around 1 pm, and the wind was so strong that we were lying on the sand with our towels wrapped around us to protect us

'MINI MOKE'

from the sand hitting our backs like forks sticking into our skin.

I remember Kerri being dumped by a huge wave, and when she gained her composure, one breast was where it should be, but the other had popped out, gasping for air. Quickly and without haste, but with a degree of embarrassment, she quickly put it back where it belonged.

Kerri also had an unwanted attachment to a blue bottle. They are not jellyfish, yet come with tentacles up to ten metres long. They appear in the summer months and can cause a major amount of pain when they sting. They have also been known to affect a person's ability to breathe as a result of the shock. I think Kerri still describes the pain as worse than childbirth, even though she had a caesarean.

And what about the torrential rain? It's a tropical climate, so there is no hiding from the inclement weather. As a child, I would trample through water in the gutters with my friend Paul, after a heavy downpour, and would embark on icy pole stick races, until we lost them down the drain. We would have been in our element in Surfers after a massive downpour. It would have been seen as the Melbourne Cup of Icy Pole racing, with the drain being the finishing post.

I mentioned earlier that there is a real lifestyle to be experienced on the Gold Coast. Somehow, motivation is easy and a new fitness regime begins as soon as you arrive at your destination. Maybe it's the weather; maybe it's the sand and surf.

The sun's rays peek through the blinds around 5 am each day, depending on the time of the year, and by 6 am, most are out on the foreshore, riding their 'Lime hire bikes,' which tend to get discarded anywhere along the path by runners and walkers, many in skimpy running gear, and that is just the men.

Melanoma heaven, you might say, as over-tanned people walk past and you wonder how long it has been since they have been to their GP for a skin check.

It is a great lifestyle, and whether it be for a jam-packed holiday, or a relaxing one, the Gold Coast, and in particular, Surfers Paradise, must be considered.

But expect the unexpected.

As I neared the end of my four kilometre morning walk, I began to look forward to my first latte of the day. Just as I bent down to stretch my weary legs, I noticed a beautifully coloured parakeet sitting on the grass. I watched it for a while and noticed it hopping over the grass, stopping when it got to the steps. It became obvious that it was having difficulty flying.

All of a sudden, it came over to where I had been sitting on the step, and jumped onto my foot; we gazed in each other's eyes. I was conscious of not picking it up, as I didn't want to cause stress.

I waited another five minutes or so, but it wouldn't move.

AUSTRALIAN PARAKEET

I googled the closest vet, which was about three kilometres down the Gold Coast Highway. They advised that there was a condition affecting parakeets that could paralyze them, and asked if I could bring it to the surgery.

It let me grasp it, although after thirty seconds started biting me and breaking my skin. I stood on the highway, holding this bird in one hand, and with the other, waving down taxis. The eight that I attracted shook their heads and wound down their windows to advise that they had other jobs. Feeling frustrated, I stood at the lights and approached each car pulling up, asking them for a ride to the vet.

Perhaps they thought I was a carjacker, but again they all advised that they were busy. I was starting to panic for this little bird, when I noticed a young couple pulling up to the lights. They wound down their window and were more than happy to drive me to the door of the vet.

As I walked in, the receptionist was just hanging up the phone and asked if I was from Cavill Avenue. She advised that she had just hung up from Wildlife Australia and they were on their way to pick up the parakeet. I hope that in some way, I have contributed to this bird having a long and healthy life. For the record, I had to walk another three kilometres back to my hotel, and it cost me $30 at the chemist, for antiseptic wash, antiseptic cream, and Band-Aids, but I wouldn't have changed it for anything.

You wouldn't believe it, but the next night, two parakeets flew onto my seventeenth-floor balcony and sat there for around five minutes. I was surprised that they could fly that HIGH, but I wonder if it was a sign.

Conclusion

Writing a book was an adventure and a challenge. I spent my life having health issues but even they were controlled. A heart attack, two brain bleeds, a double heart bypass, ten hernias, a pacemaker, and 172 tablets per week. I was able to accept all these challenges. What I failed to accept were the challenges I was experiencing inside my head that couldn't be seen. As I neared retirement, I felt that I had achieved everything I could have and had been quite successful after working very hard. However, I felt that I couldn't add value to my life or to the value of others anymore. I researched how, where, and when I could end it all. My mind was made up. I had no reason to live. No sense of purpose. Just before reaching my planned date, I accepted my psychiatrist's advice and went into hospital for five weeks, receiving ECT treatment (electro-convulsive therapy) and time away from depression triggers. Apart from the reconfiguring of my brain, I think the five weeks of living in a protected bubble gave me the confidence to talk out loud about my disease. By accident, I discovered that I had many funny travel stories stored in my brain. After writing this book, I now have a sense of purpose. A reason to live, and an excitement to continue living. My goal here was to make you laugh, albeit at our expense. I hope that happened. If at any stage you question your value to society, seek help because you never know what hidden talents you have and how your life can be reinvented.

The book has not pleased everyone. My wife, Kerri, now questions whether we should ever go on holidays again, considering all of the things that have gone wrong, and my daughter, Tara, is still not talking to me for mentioning the time she projectile vomited in Penang.

Acknowledgments

Thank you must go to Iain Watson, Mandy Crane, Jana Frawley, David Borean, Kerri, Tara, and the many friends and family who provided feedback on my work and support through my challenging times.

About Atmosphere Press

Founded in 2015, Atmosphere Press was built on the principles of Honesty, Transparency, Professionalism, Kindness, and Making Your Book Awesome. As an ethical and author-friendly hybrid press, we stay true to that founding mission today.

If you're a reader, enter our giveaway for a free book here:

SCAN TO ENTER
BOOK GIVEAWAY

If you're a writer, submit your manuscript for consideration here:

SCAN TO SUBMIT
MANUSCRIPT

And always feel free to visit Atmosphere Press and our authors online at atmospherepress.com. See you there soon!

About the Author

ALLAN BRODIE lives in Melbourne, Australia, with his very tolerant wife of over four decades, Kerri, his beautiful daughter, Tara, and their energetic toy poodle, Ivy. A committed sports fan, Allan is one of the few people to see his beloved Australian Rules football team, St. Kilda, win their only premiership in the club's 150-year history.

Allan had a successful career in media advertising before taking the new path of author, making use of his travel experiences and exquisite quirky humour to let readers journey through the world with a smile on their faces. When not writing (or doing the housework), he devotes his time to volunteering at an animal rescue facility.